CW00429939

Chaos Streams 01

First edition 2016

ISBN: 978-0-9954904-4-4

Published by The Universe Machine, Norwich.

"We live in a rainbow of chaos."
Paul Cézanne

Contents

All artworks by Frater Alvph Draconis, excepting photographs and diagrams.

Opening the Temple
Sator Julian

Here are stories from modern magicians, essays, examples of ritual praxis, art and more. The authors are members of an international network of occultists called The Magical Pact of the Illuminates of Thanateros or IOT. Founded in the late 1970s this collaborative project (hence 'Pact') of magical practitioners is predicated on group magical work, primarily of the face-to-face (rather than virtual) variety. For me this was its attraction when I undertook the IOT training program some fifteen years ago and was subsequently initiated into that organisation.

My first experience of group esoteric practice, decades before I encountered the IOT, was in the context of experimental Wicca. I've always enjoyed the learning, the camaraderie, the challenge and the possibilities inherent in collaborative occultism. Humans are social creatures and, for me, the delight of exploring The Mystery (those 'occulted' aspects of ourselves and the outer universe) in company with others is tremendous. This is especially the case when it comes to ceremonial work. Having a group of friends who are experienced magicians to work alongside of, is a priceless gift. As a member of the IOT I'm presented with just such a socio-esoteric laboratory, which permits experiments that simply wouldn't be possible without other practitioners. I can learn from my peers; their observations, innovations, failings and successes. I can find myself encountering knowledgeable individuals schooled in systems I would perhaps never have chanced upon in my solitary studies. I can observe, over time, the group intelligence and culture, and find myself uplifted by one of the core ideas of the IOT, namely that we all have the potential to be amazing magicians.

A minimal and intentionally subverted decision making system exists within the IOT, and at international through to individual levels, the Pact is a series of requests and agreements. For this reason it is impossible for 'The IOT' to say anything as a total organization (beyond the organisational structure outlined in *The Book of the Pact*, which is an evolving and regularly reviewed set of guidelines). So while all the authors in this book are IOT initiates this collection cannot be said to be some kind of 'official communication' (in that late 19th century style of quasi-Masonic esoteric Orders). While maintaining a framework of roles and responsibilities the autonomy of the individual magicians is key to the successful functioning of the IOT. Each person, from very early on in their engagement with the Pact, is encouraged (with specific support from their Mentor) to present their own Work in a group setting. Members of the IOT must be sufficiently interested in the idea of group occult practice to lead rituals, and to become skilled in sharing technique and teachings with others.

Pursuing a particular aspect of occult praxis (be that rune magic, Discordian performance, Tai Chi, Lovecraftian Evocation etc), learning how to share this in group context, and using that opportunity to enhance one's own magical unfolding (aka 'spiritual development') and that of one's peers—that's the raison d'être of the Pact. The IOT is a community of practice, a *Sangha* to use Buddhist terminology.

Meanwhile the approach that has become known as 'chaos magic' (in a nutshell; the active use and celebration of multiple models of magiculture) has of course spread far beyond the IOT. Indeed this chaoist or 'eclectic approach' is now the default style of many magical practitioners. While there are folks who enjoy reconstructionist approaches to magic (be they derived from Germanic, Ancient Egyptian or other cultural contexts), most people now realise that 'tradition' is mostly in the mind of the beholder. The unpicking by insider researchers such as Ronald Hutton of the romantic Margaret Murray inspired history of Witchcraft, and the pervasive insights of postmodern philosophy, mean that even the most dyed-in-the-woad reconstructionist should (albeit grudgingly) recognise that concepts such as lineage, initiated secrets, 'the old ways' and all that are actually constantly in a state of flux and re-creation. We are all magpies in one way or another, and we're all of us making it up as we go along.

Within the broader sangha of postmodern 'chaos magic' occultism there exists a variety of networks, and nowadays many of these are digitally mediated gatherings in virtual space. Probably one of the best ways to get a feel for the cultural landscape of contemporary chaos magic(k) is to explore the social media spaces dedicated to its discussion and, critically, practice.

The virtual networks of Z-Cluster, the online archive of chaosmatrix.org ('Immanentizing the Eschaton since 27th October 1995") and many other virtual spaces have been a natural habitat of chaos magicians for many years. Using these virtual spaces to allow magicians—who may be geographically distant—to collaborate, seems to come easily to this community. Finding ways to do shared esoteric practice using virtual spaces is a burgeoning, and in my opinion, exciting field as occulture enters the second decade of the 21st century.

The development of this new context is something I'm very aware of. When I was a teenager I had to go to physical libraries, furtively read through the occult books collection, eventually buy underground Pagan 'zines and slowly make contact with the occult community of my island. Today there are no such barriers for many people in the networked world. Now the issue is not lack of information so much as the need for the aspiring magician to learn to sift the wheat from the online chaff. Considered symbolically, my journey into magic was one of the quest; seeking out the hidden and rare, whereas today students perhaps follow an alchemical narrative, refining the gold from a world wide web replete with dross.

In this new techno-mediated occulture people rightly question the need for old style quasi-Masonic magickal Orders. As well as rightly distrusting their apparently inflexible hierarchical structures, pompous sounding grades (with those ostensible assumptions of magical superiority and inferiority) and all that other bullshit, some doubt whether these structures have any value within our computer connected, virtual sangha.

Many of the old school Orders, as well as The Pact of the IOT, are being, and should be, influenced by these important cultural changes in occulture. The details of the Order style of network are likely to reform, hopefully to become more 'open source' (for example by offering opportunities for people who are not formally members to participate in rituals, collaborative work, retreats and so forth). Elements such as a training program (which everyone follows just to ensure that members have a common baseline level of familiarity with core techniques), and initiation (formally saying 'I'd like to contribute to this group process') are likely to remain basic requirements. These things matter because groups such as the IOT, while they have virtual expressions, are primarily about doing face-to-face group magic with other people. To maintain the integrity of those spaces, their safety and power, it's important to be able to screen people for their commitment and suitability. Formulating a group boundary so that, collectively, the network can include people who are a good fit with the Pact's culture. It's necessary to provide mentoring and support systems that foster an individual's progress and autonomy, as well as our collective intelligence, and it's vital to create spaces where physical group magic can take place (in the case of the IOT this means physical Working Group and Temple meetings, Section Moots and the international Annual General Meeting).

But in all this organisational chatter, what really matters is the people.

Personally I'm privileged to be on excellent terms with folk from many traditions; druids, Setians, native shamans, Initiates of The Ordo Templi Orientis, Freemasons, radical Goddess feminists and others. I'm met many fabulous people in the magical culture I inhabit, and I've found a very high density of fabulousness within the IOT.

When I stand in a circle with these people and look around at my Brothers, Sisters and Sators* I am amazed. It's like being in a graphic novel. Here are these heroes of practice, each one with amazing abilities. We are an assembly of archetypal forces. In part this is a consequence of my relationship, over many years, with these other magicians and I'm sure members of many other esoteric groups get a similar buzz at their gatherings. For me the people of the IOT provide a wonderful community of research, experiment, morphing 'tradition', fellowship, support and of course, laughter.

While a few people stay with the process for many years there are many, many more who come into the IOT, benefit from that space, and who move on to pastures new. There are many occultists out there who have been members of the IOT and have encountered a new style or approach in that setting, and then go on to pursue that in more depth outside of the Pact setting. There are some who return years later to the IOT circle, bringing with them the experiences they have gained. The Pact acts as an experimental space, ideal for people who have come to some kind of spiritual and/or personal crossroads, and for many it is pivotal in their journey of Illumination (as the essay 'What Has the Pact Done for Me?' in this collection makes explicit).

Unless a person violates the trust of the IOT, and there is a consensus on their exclusion (a very rare situation), former members, even though they are no longer 'active' remain Initiates**. In this way the IOT maintains connections with people in many different traditions, some of whom are former active members.

The IOT remains an evolving, flexible but remarkably stable system. The number of members has remained relatively constant for many years and this is to be expected. Anthropologists tell us that the average size of a human tribe is around 150 people and, since the IOT privileges face-to-face group magical interaction, it makes sense that the figures for membership echo (in different geographical regions) that kind of scale.

Today the IOT is old enough that there are Members who have a family lineage within the Pact. Thus this organisation grows, matures and changes, adapting to its place in an occulture where virtual collaboration is possible and where physical group practice, supported by a training program and the wider international network, remains essential. The Pact remains a space that people interested in group experiments in chaos magic can access across the globe.

You cannot step into the same stream twice, as Heraclitus wisely observed. However you can plunge in and see how it feels to you in this moment. This collection of essays is, in a sense, how it feels to be part of the IOT, at least for the contributors to this book; they are both representative of, and responses to, the Pact, but by no means the whole picture; remember kids, nothing may be absolutely true, and anything may prove possible.

I hope you enjoy dipping into these streams of chaos.

* 'Sator' is the gender inclusive pronoun rather than Frater (Brother) or Soror (Sister). The collective noun 'sibling' is often used in the IOT to refer to other Members.

** This is the case in the British Isles Section of the IOT. Other Sections are autonomous, and may have different cultures and policies.

Chaos Magic - a Brief History
Frater Ahperl

THE SCEPTIC'S WAY

As with most things which seem remote in time, it's difficult to pin down exactly when it all started. Chaos Magic is not a system invented by a single magical writer, but a whole approach to magic, the kind of movement within the history of magic that is often referred to as a current. A current is a novel way of talking about magic, and the Chaos Magic current emerged in the 1970s, influenced by writings that stretch back a decade or two before that.

As far as I know, the first publication to use the term Chaos Magic was Pete Carroll's *Liber Null* (1), the second red cover edition by Ray Sherwin's Morton Press (1978-79). But the core idea that the Chaos current grew from is that we are not stuck with a single belief about the world, but that radically different beliefs about what is going on can be entertained within the same skull.

Before this kind of thinking, magic had been in the doldrums for some years, with a tendency to reduce everything to psychological models. The reason for this is clear—a population increasingly educated to a scientific worldview had no room for magic in their belief-worlds, so magic retreated to the esoteric end of psychology. Even a giant of scientific imagination such as Einstein found it too big a leap to believe in some aspects of quantum mechanics because they implied the possibility of 'spooky action at a distance.' No-one brought up and encultured in the modern world can easily bring themselves to believe in magic, and this includes people who've grown up in the depths of the Amazon forest. In the course of interviewing visionary artist and ex-ayahuasquero Pablo Amaringo, Donal Ruane asked him if he believed in the spirits all the time, even when not under the influence of ayahuasca (2). No, replied Amaringo, even shamans can't believe in the spirits all the time, not in the modern world.

Chaos Magic attracted me and many others because it does not require that you abandon scientific thinking. Rather, you grow accustomed to switching between viewpoints, depending on which is the most relevant and useful for what you want to achieve. So it's OK to 'believe in' say, subtle energies if that is what it takes for you to get results in that area. After your energy magic practice, you can go back to the physics-based view that there is no evidence for such energies. Chaos Magic was the first approach to magic that faced up to the challenge of culturally-ingrained scepticism.

MULTIPLE MODELS

Multi-model thinking as a way of accommodating the existence of magic seems to have originated with Robert Anton Wilson, who called it *multi-model agnosticism,* since the core idea is not to hold on to any belief, but to admit that one really does not know any ultimate truth. Any perspective we have on the world is bound to be part of a massive, inclusive gestalt, a whole bunch of beliefs about the world that come as a complete nested set, every belief implying every other. These sets of world-describing (or world-creating) beliefs are known as *reality tunnels*. Once we recognize that we are in a particular reality tunnel which limits everything we can think—for instance Atheist Scientism, Buddhism or Catholicism—we are then free to shift to another. This is an essential skill for any magician to master who values their mental health in the modern or postmodern age. Applied to magic, multi-model thinking went way beyond what the post-Crowley current called Thelema was doing with belief. It was radical, in the genuine sense, looking right into the roots of magical technique.

In this kind of thinking Wilson acknowledged his debt to Discordianism, a spoof on religion (or a spoof religion) centred round the identification of Eris, Greek goddess of Chaos and Discord, as the true mistress of reality, the most relevant deity for a world whose chaos was becoming more visible year by media-enhanced year. The Ur-text of Discordianism, first released in 1963, was *Principia Discordia, Or How I Found Goddess and What I Did To Her When I Found Her,* by Malaclypse the Younger (Greg Weddell) and Lord Omar Khayyam Ravenshurst (Kerry Thornley) (3). It brought a disrespectful scepticism to matters of religion and philosophy, and its playful approach to belief provided the spirit, though not yet the worked-out details, for the multi-model approach. Many of the ideas and characters in the *Principia* were dramatized and developed in fictional form in the novel *Illuminatus!,* by Robert Shea and Robert Anton Wilson (4).

Illuminatus! was the first novel I read which explicitly depicted *magic actually happening in a believable world*, not as a fantasy in some world where magic is much more common, like Discworld or Hogwarts or any of the fabled lands of sword and sorcery. Here was magic leaking into the real world! Here was a narrative which tempted us to consider that *magic might actually be real*, and I took the bait, allowing myself to believe just that, for the first time in my life. *Illuminatus!* achieved this literary trick by using multiple viewpoints within the same character—a person may think in magical terms, then switch to physics or police procedure—foreshadowing Wilson's explicit adoption of multi-modal agnosticism (MMA) in books such as *The Cosmic Trigger* (5).

So the scene was set for the explicit application of MMA to magic. One of the earliest avowedly magical books to challenge and dismantle belief was Ramsey Dukes/Lionel Snell's *SSOTBME* (1974) (6). This book was possibly the first to present magically the idea of viewing life through different belief systems. Dukes outlined four basic ways of apprehending the world: Science, Art, Religion and Magic. These correspond to the Platonic trinity of Truth, Beauty and Goodness, with the addition of Wholeness.

Here's a version of that four quadrant scheme, which we will find useful later.

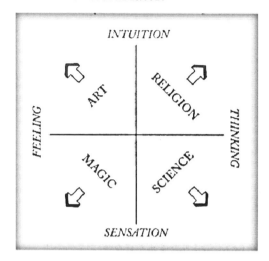

Dukes leads us into elegant and entertaining deconstructions of beliefs that people hold about all sorts of aspects of life. This intellectual fluidity produces something close to the Socratic *aporia*, a pathlessness, an awareness that all beliefs are so questionable that the reader is left floating in a void. An amusing void, and rather exciting. It was perhaps inevitable that someone would then come along and form these ideas into something that could be used in practical magic. That person was Pete Carroll. However, to understand the streams of ideas that make up Chaos Magic there's somewhere else we need to look first.

WILLIAM BURROUGHS, NOTHING IS TRUE AND THE '23 CURRENT'

If you've read anything about Chaos Magic you will probably have come across the slogan 'Nothing is

True, Everything is Permitted,' bandied about with varying degrees of irony. In the sound-piece *Apocalypse* (7) Burroughs intones: 'Everything is permitted BECAUSE nothing is true... It is all make-believe, illusion, dream, art.' This nihilism is a dramatization of the way we make up our worlds, an exposure of the inherent fictional qualities of the realities we each inhabit.

This phrase came into the Chaos Magic stream on the same wavelength as the '23 enigma', another part of the Chaos picture you're bound to have come across. Both of these Burroughs elements entered Chaos via Robert Anton Wilson. His novel *Illuminatus!* contains elements of a linearly-laid-out simplification of Burroughs's conspiracy nightmare universe, in which occasionally superconscious secret agents in deep cover as social lowlifes struggle against overlapping alien control agencies embedded in human language and neurology. The 23 pattern was originally picked up by Burroughs, who told RAW that he had known a sea captain called Clark who bragged that he had been sailing 23 years without an accident. That very day, Clark's ship did have an accident, which killed him and everyone else aboard. As Burroughs was digesting this news the same evening, he learned from a radio news report of the crash of an airliner in the USA. The pilot was another Captain Clark and the flight was Flight 23. From that day, Burroughs looked out for the number 23 turning up in weird situations, particularly deadly ones, and found many. In 1993, four years before his death, Burroughs joined the Illuminates of Thanateros, not as an honoured subcultural elder, but as an active member who worked all the exercises and contributed rituals which were networked to other members.

The '23 enigma' as Wilson called it, is notorious for sweeping people up into related synchronicities. In February 1996 I went with two other chaos magicians to visit William Burroughs at his home in Lawrence, Kansas. We'd been running a three-day magical meeting and we flew, in that wide-open state that comes from magical intensity and sleep-deprivation, from Seattle to Kansas City. We boarded the plane, and the captain introduced himself as... Captain Clark! There was more than a frisson of mortal dread mingled with the sheer euphoria of synchronicity as the plane soared up into what looked like a storm front.

Chaos Magic has a strong anti-authoritarian and anti-establishment bias, so it became the favoured magical model of what we might call the magical underground. This facet owes a lot to the above strand in the history of Chaos, a strand we could call the '23 Current.' This type of practitioner, the urban anarchist fictionalized and mythicized in Grant Morrison's *The Invisibles*, is one type of Chaos Magician. Another type of Chaos Magician is the practitioner who pops up at big social events to stir up some community magic. This kind of magical activity is quite distinct from the usual formal elitism of occult orders and tends towards a festive, open, socially-inclusive approach to magic, modelled on an imagining of a kind of village shamanism.

A third kind of practitioner is happy to work their way through the exercises of a formal order. This kind of hermetic, more insular approach came to the fore as Carroll crystallized MMA into the technical discipline of Chaos Magic. At this point, part of the current veered away from the festive and towards the hermetic.

PHASE 1: CORE TECHNICAL IDEAS: CARROLL, SHERWIN AND THE EARLY IOT

Chaos Magic crystallized as a current with the publication of two books in 1978, both issued by Ray Sherwin's Morton Press. Sherwin's own *The Book of Results* (8) was a small booklet with a set of instructions for doing your own sigils, with minimal metaphysics. It no doubt encouraged a lot of people to have a go at making up their own magical spells. Years later the occultural organization Thee Temple Ov Psychick Youth was adopting this technology in their monthly sigil-fests. (In fact TOPY Steel, the Sheffield 'station,' reissued Sherwin's books in the early 1990s.) The other 1978 publication was Pete Carroll's *Liber Null*. This was a full technically-slanted articulation of the multi-model approach, and at its centre was a major insight into what magic needs in order to succeed. Carroll articulated two ingredients essential to all spell-casting—belief shifting and what he called *gnosis*.

The idea of *belief itself as a magical technique* is the core of Chaos Magic's technical innovation, its technical USP. In magic, we choose a belief or, more often, a nested set of beliefs, that makes the result we want possible or, when the magic succeeds, *inevitable*.

To view belief as a major principle of magic is a very powerful belief-about-belief, or meta-belief, as central a magical principle as, for instance, Crowley's idea of True Will. Julian Vayne, in *Now That's What I Call Chaos Magick* (co-authored with Greg Humphries) sketches a history of modern magic which I would broadly agree with, particularly in the way he teases out central principles from a succession of magical texts. Starting with Eliphas Levi, who gave us Will, the Astral Light and Correspondences, via the Golden Dawn with Imagination and Aleister Crowley who enjoined us to Work Without Lust of Result we come to Austin Spare's rejection of traditional systems and embrace of Open-Handed Magic, based on a DIY-metaphysics.

Some of these powerful magical ideas are also some of the ancestors of Chaos Magic. Carroll's core ideas, Belief Shifting and Gnosis, are at this level of insight into the mechanisms of magic, especially Belief. Carroll has written a lot more on magic since *Liber Null*, much of it original and interesting, but nothing that has anywhere near this level of insight and magico-historical significance.

The technology of Belief is of course a child of MMA, or even a facet of it. What's more, magicians need some degree of MMA to even get started in doing magic. Let's face it, magic is an undertaking that is right out on the fringe, where the DSM, the Bible of psychiatry, tells us we are nuts even to entertain notions so far outside the mainstream. In deciding you are a magician, you have already used the power of belief in a way very few people do. When you do a ritual, you are engaging in what Ray Sherwin identified in *The Theatre of Magic* (1982) (9) as a piece of theatre designed to shift your reality out of the mundane and facilitate your magic. When you are in your temple/sacred grove you are engaging in the nested beliefs a) that you are a magician, b) that tonight you are a Qabalistic/Celtic magician and c) whatever specific belief shift will enable the spell to work. (And maybe a couple more, just for fun!)

Our beliefs about the world, our narratives, our reality-tunnels, can be difficult to let go of and replace with new ones. This is where the second principle, gnosis, comes in. What Carroll called gnosis is more often called an Altered State of Consciousness or ASC. I prefer Extraordinary State of Consciousness. This is the psychic lube that enables us to slip from one reality to another, dissolving the resistance of our old narratives and delivering us into our chosen worlds.

Gathering up the strands of early Chaos Magic, we can see another principle, which came more into focus in the later stages: an overarching pragmatic philosophy of *if it works use it*. Any techniques and concepts can be 'dragooned into service,' whether they have good magical pedigrees or not. More on this later.

A GLIMPSE OF SOME EARLY CHAOS WORKINGS

Those two 1978 books, *Liber Null* and *The Book of Results*, seeded the interest that led to the formation of the first IOT groups, notably in Yorkshire. Chaos Magic's early upsurge in that part of the world is due partly to the presence of The Sorcerer's Apprentice occult supply shop in Leeds. In the late 1970s the S.A. held Saturday coffee mornings where, amongst other mages, I met Ray Sherwin and Pete Carroll. The other significant contribution in those early days was from Ray Sherwin, who often invited other young magicians to his house in East Morton, which meetings eventually led to the formation of two Chaos Magic groups, including the so-called Circle of Chaos, which ran for just over three years with a core of eight members.

The rituals in that era were experiments in 'paradigm shifting'—Egyptian, Norse, Celtic, and science fiction theatres, together with considerable research into what gnoses worked best. We tried chanting, dancing, esoteric bodywork, walking on the moors on a moonless night, suspension in a harness, shock and fear, poetic beauty and of course psychedelic sacraments. There are those who, in order to make Chaos Magic conform to their own predilections, would deny this latter influence, but it is illustrated by an occasion when another member of the Circle of Chaos and I went through the whole of the group diary, near the end of that group's existence, and counted the proportion of rites which used psychedelic sacraments: it was exactly half. Not only that, but our most original, successful and powerful working—the creation of the egregore entity mentioned below—was performed on an LSD sacrament.

Looking back to those times, between 1984 and 1987, I am struck by how the content of the group's work changed. At first it was all about invoking deities to gain their qualities and powers. Only later did we focus on results in the outer world, and our greatest working was without a doubt the creation of an egregore-entity, a kind of mega-servitor to do our wills. This entity marked a new level of magical success for those in the group.

PHASE 2: BROADENING: URBAN SHAMANISM AND PAINTING IT BLACK

The second wave of Chaos Magic had at its core a broadening of models. The earliest sign of this new current was Phil Hine's *Urban Shaman* trilogy (10). These little books, published while Phil was running the ground-breaking *Pagan News* magazine, painted a picture of a modern urban magician navigating the currents of modern urban life. The practitioner reaches back to the earliest conceptions of the magician as community shaman while using urban reality itself as a symbol system, decoding the signs of the city like her remote ancestor decoded the language of the forest. This was a new glamour that many people found more inspiring than what had gone before, and broadened the base of appeal of Chaos Magic.

This broadening and reaching out into new areas developed into a phase of 'paint it black and stick a chaosphere on it'—in other words, mining both magical and non-magical techniques for anything that could be of use in empowering our magic. Two examples are the psychological tricks of NLP, and the deep sensed-energy gnosis and healing power of Connected Breathwork.

Some people hated this aspect of Chaos Magic. I remember picking up some occult mag in the mid-90s and reading an article which went off on a rant about

Chaos Magicians 'dragooning' everything into the service of their magic. I think that's rather a good expression, and I have no shame at all about using it. Ian Read once said: 'Magicians are wolves of the spirit.' I'm happy with that; we take what we need to do our wills, whatever it is disguised as. The writer of the article was presumably one of those people who has a purity problem—magic is something separate from the rest of life and must maintain its pristine, unsullied obscurity.

PHASE 3: ART IN THE PUBLIC EYE: THE HYPERSIGIL

In the mid-1990s Grant Morrison created the graphic novel series *The Invisibles* (11), a tale of magically-powered anarchists struggling against the forces of political evil. He declared later that the whole series had been a *hypersigil*, which basically means an entire work of art with a magical purpose or purposes. In 1997 I sent some promo about my new book *Chaotopia!* to Morrison's publishers in New York. Two weeks later I was home briefly from work and the phone rang, Grant Morrison calling from Glasgow to tell me he already had the book. It was becoming clear that Chaos Magic now had an artistic dimension, out there in view of the public.

PHASE 4: BROADER STILL AND MAYBE DEEPER: *CHAOTOPIA!* AND *NOW THAT'S WHAT I CALL CHAOS MAGICK.*

In 1997 when I wrote *Chaotopia!* (12) I knew that Chaos Magic needed to address areas that had so far been sidelined. Previously, I'd always been put off mysticism by the religious viruses inhabiting most mystical discourse but now, rather than just being the go-to technical approach to magic, Chaos needed to take in mysticism and the pursuit of so-called higher consciousness. I wanted to see Chaos uncouple these issues from religion and treat them as subjective-experimental disciplines, in the same way it took in results-oriented magic and make more sense out of them for the modern age.

Chaotopia! was a book of essays structured around the Timothy Leary and RA Wilson 'Eight Circuits' model of consciousness. Deliberately loose and open-ended, the book was a hypersigil to manifest the same kind of critical approach to mysticism as Chaos Magic had done with magic.

The same idea was growing in other minds too. Julian Vayne's *Now That's What I Call Chaos Magick* (2004, co-authored with Greg Humphries) (13) contained reports from the inner spaces of magical endeavour, the vital nourishing subjectivity of the magician's life, including reports on Vayne's personal method of invoking the Holy Guardian Angel, using that valuable concept whilst ditching the dodgy metaphysics.

My hypersigil succeeded. First came Alan Chapman's *Advanced Magick for Beginners* (14) in 2008, laying out magic in a way which related its practice explicitly to Awakening, and making the idea of Awakening much more believable for many people, including myself.

And then in 2011 came an even more radical deconstruction of what magic is about, Aaron Daniels' *Imaginal Reality* (15), finally updating Chaos Magic's philosophical basis to take in existentialism, and developing a full-on mystical-existentialist approach to the Magical Quest.

This was the peak of the Fourth Wave, and is about where the current stood a few years ago. Here is an attempt at an historical overview.

THREE FLAVOURS OF CHAOS

Magic is a personal art. It has a few features which lend some aspects of it to a scientific treatment, and even some core principles which are sufficiently robust to be thought of as 'laws', but these are very few indeed. Recalling Ramsey Dukes' four quadrants (see above), we can expect Magic to be coloured on one side by Science, and on the other by Art. As far as the 'Science model' of magic goes, most of the core principles were mentioned above, under 'Phase 1', and this list—updated to read Will, Symbols and Correspondences, Imagination, Working Without Lust of Result, Open-Handed Magic, Gnosis and Belief—represents pretty much the full extent of that model's historical development so far; I doubt there is much more that can currently be said about magic's most general principles.

On the Art side, we tend to get more pragmatism—in the Art model, we are not so concerned with universal principles but rather each of us picks personal methods and symbols based on personal magical effectiveness and expresses them through Art.

A third position rounds out the picture—the 'Meta-View.' This is a return to the original perspectives of Chaos, the MMA-based approach that never loses sight of the fact that the magical scheme you've adopted for your working is just that, something you've chosen whilst fully aware there is no absolute truth to it.

Let's look at where a few of the major Chaos writings fall in this tripartite scheme.

THE SCIENCE MODEL

Pete Carroll was the first to apply the MMA Meta-View to magical technique, in *Liber Null*. In subsequent works he has turned increasingly away from the Meta-View towards the building of finalized, detailed systems, starting with the Equations of Magic, which I have never heard of anyone using to plan a spell, and culminating in the exhaustive psychocosm of *EPOCH*. It seems to me that such obsessive scientism can only end in an essentially decadent approach (see my review of *EPOCH*, (16)), because magic is much more than a system when it is fluid and adaptable. Also, other people's systems are inherently limiting to any but the absolute beginner in magic who may need a ready-made psychocosm as a 'starter kit', an example to follow. Spare would have agreed with William Blake when he wrote: 'I must Create a System or be enslaved by another man's; I will not reason and compare: my business is to create.'

Another problem for those who would reduce Magic to Science is that, as the theorist becomes increasingly convinced that they have found permanent, rock-solid principles they tend to reject all the stuff that no longer works for them, on the basis that therefore it can no longer work for anyone else. This confusion of personal style with overarching principle is a serious drawback to the scientific-reductionist approach.

After the 'Urban Shaman' trilogy Phil Hine's books become a little science-like, with their reliance on psychology, especially of the self-help variety. However, his use of the Meta-View is transparent and clear.

THE ART MODEL

Austin Osman Spare is, of course, the exemplary artist-magician. His magical world, as revealed in *The Book of Pleasure* (17) is intensely personal, but also advocates the DIY approach which opens up the possibility of a meta-view, because Spare teaches us how to make up our own systems.

There are fewer 'pure' examples of the Art Model of magic in book form than there are of the other two perspectives, because artists often do their magic without writing much about it. Nathaniel Harris's work is definitely in the Art zone, and we can probably include Julian Wilde's *Grimoire of Chaos Magic* too. Andrieh Vitimus's *Hands On Chaos Magic* (18) has something of the Art approach in its ruthlessly-inclusive pragmatism and exposition of a personal current of magic, and also much of the Meta View, implied of course by such a wide-ranging collection of magical styles.

The best-known magical writer to address this issue is Alan Moore. Moore is not an avowed Chaos Magician but is obviously very close to that current, and he has written and spoken extensively on the idea that there is basically no difference between art and magic. This is a useful approach for the magical artist—everything they create is a hypersigil—but applied as a blanket truth about magic it is a massive overstatement which leaves many questions unanswered.

THE META VIEW

Just as Chaos Magic started off from the Meta View of MMA, its most radical developments also sit in that corner of the triangle. Aaron Daniels's *Imaginal Reality* may be the deepest deconstruction of magic written for a very long time, and it relies on a considerable flexibility of belief. It is impossibly difficult to imagine a Science model writer such as Carroll writing a book such as this.

CONCLUSION

Chaos Magic has, so far, been extraordinarily successful. The magical scene from the death of Crowley to the late 1970s (leaving aside the magically-influenced *cults* that mushroomed in the 60s–70s) seemed to have retreated into a Jung-influenced psychologism—'It's all in the mind (or spirit)'—with its tendency to treat magic, even from the inside, as an elder, an unrespectable uncle, now partially-rehabilitated, of psychotherapy. Magical orders were of little help—the OTO seemed to throw out anyone who was at all creative or who practised any magic outside of a few Crowley-approved rituals. Along with some vaguely neo-traditionalist yearnings, this mishmash crystallized (pun intended) into the sloppy, muddled thinking of the New Age movement. To this tired, enfeebled state of affairs

Chaos Magic opposed a vigorous, rigorous and pragmatic wizardry, a path of power whose core was the restored romance of sorcery.

This approach has been immensely influential; it would be hard to find an area of modern magical practice where its profound technical insights haven't been incorporated, though perhaps grudgingly and covertly in some instances! Chaos Magic achieved these things because of the Meta View. It must be obvious from the above that that's the view I champion, with due respect to the Science model, as long as it makes useful connections and supplies good technique and not blinkers, and an increasing feeling that my own magic is basically Art.

Chaos Magic is no guarantor of magical freedom, but in stripping magic back to its essentials it not only faced and overcame the problem of culturally-ingrained scepticism but also partakes of what I believe is a very ancient attitude to magic: radical pragmatism. Traditionalist purists often miss out on the extreme likelihood that our magical ancestors did not care about writing a book of rules but would have grasped and pressed into service anything they could get to work for them.

We can see this process in action today, by looking at the Mestizo shamanism of the Amazon basin. The violent assault of Catholicism on these tribal cultures did not weaken the magical culture of the *ayahuasqueros* but may actually have strengthened it, (19) providing them with some powerful new spirits to use in their magic.

It is possible that these highly syncretic sorcerers had among their number people who wanted to write it all down and turn it into a science. Such an activity may generate fame but it is not the most vital part of any magical current; it is basically a decadent phase, a limb of still water that will eventually stagnate into a dead end. Chaos works best in uncertainty and insecurity, where creative imagination and flexibility of belief are the most important skills.

And this of course is the ragged realm of the real world, the endlessly-mutating Chaotopia of over-lapping spheres of creation, each centred on a person or a network. In this 'Chaos of the Normal,' as Spare called it, the communitarian and cultural-transformative strands appear to be resurging, after some years in the doldrums, with the recent revival of Discordianism as a spiritual/magical backbone to a re-invented counterculture (20). Things are looking very interesting…

(1) *Liber Null* by Peter J. Carroll, https://www.amazon.co.uk/Liber-Null-Psychonaut-Peter-Carroll/dp/0877286396

(2) Donal Ruane, unpublished film interview

(3) *Principia Discordia,* free download at http://www.principiadiscordia.com/downloads/Princi pia%20Discordia.pdf

(4) *Illuminatus!* Free at http://www.integralbook.com/wp-content/uploads/2012/03/Wilson-Robert-Anton-Illuminatus-Trilogy.pdf

(5) *Cosmic Trigger Vol 1* by Robert Anton Wilson, https://www.amazon.co.uk/Cosmic-Trigger-Final-Secret-Illuminati/dp/1561840033

(6) *SSOTBME*
http://darkbooks.org/pp.php?v=1161598070

(7) Apocalypse,
https://www.youtube.com/watch?v=bubCpbx-DHk

(8) *The Book of Results* by Ray Sherwin,
https://www.amazon.co.uk/Book-Results-Ray-Sherwin/dp/1411625587

(9) *The Theatre of Magic* by Ray Sherwin
http://www.philhine.org.uk/writings/pdfs/theatre.pdf

(10) Phil Hine's *Urban Shaman* trilogy - download from http://www.holybooks.com/techniques-of-modern-shamanism-vol-1-3-by-phil-hine/.

(11) *The Invisibles*
https://www.amazon.co.uk/Invisibles-Say-you-Want-Revolution/dp/1852867213

(12) *Chaotopia!* by Dave Lee,
http://www.chaotopia.com/publications/

(13) *NTWICCM* https://www.amazon.co.uk/Thats-What-Call-Chaos-Magick/dp/1869928741

(14) Alan Chapman's *Advanced Magick for Beginners* https://www.amazon.co.uk/Advanced-Magick-Beginners-Alan-Chapman/dp/1904658415

(15) *Imaginal Reality*,
https://www.amazon.com/Imaginal-Reality-Aaron-B-Daniels/dp/1904658490

(16) http://chaotopia-dave.blogspot.co.uk/2015/01/review-of-epoch-by-peter-j-carroll-and.html

(17) *The Book of Pleasure* by AO Spare, https://www.amazon.co.uk/Book-Pleasure-Self-love-Psychology-Ecstasy/dp/187218958X

(18) Andrieh Vitimus - *Hands On Chaos Magic*, https://www.amazon.co.uk/Hands-Chaos-Magic-Reality-Manipulation/dp/0738715085

(19) http://www.ayahuasca.com/ayahuasca-overviews/unraveling-the-mystery-of-the-origin-of-ayahuasca/

(20) http://www.vice.com/en_uk/read/the-discordian-revival-chaos-festival

Live Chaos

Frater Biqfus

EXPERIENCES

It's early on a Spring evening, broad daylight. Three men sit drinking cider on a bench at the edge of a gigantic island roundabout in South London. They are about to discover they have front-row seats for an unusual performance.

Five figures approach from one of the four roads radiating from the island. Four of them are in black hoodies, but the fifth wears a spectacularly-horned goat's head, a black, winged cape and three rows of shiny rubber breasts. The figures assemble on one of the three grassy mounds on the island, a city planner's take on the round barrows, where ancestors keep watch over the intersections of arterial tracks. The group proceed to chant barbarous words. They are calling on the beast-god/dess Baphomet to manifest, here in this eye at the centre of roaring, circling streams of traffic.

We were in London for an exhibition of the magical art of Austin Osman Spare. And after our Baphomet working, we made a pilgrimage to one of Spare's many South London residences, on the nearby Tabard Garden Estate. Sitting on the brick walls of the flowerbeds in the central square, we made offerings of beer and tobacco to the memory and spirit of AOS. Two large, friendly tabby cats then approached us. They looked exactly like I imagine the descendants of Spare's 'Tigers' would look.

Rituals in public have a special power, partly because of the special qualities of the place itself in which the ritual occurs, partly derived from the sheer strangeness of working more-or-less theatrical magic in public, and partly because there's a real risk of getting the wrong kind of attention.

Our next scene is the ancient city centre of York. It's mid-evening on Halloween weekend. Fourteen black-robed men and women file along silently by the city walls and into the centre. Children jeer and throw eggs, but from a considerable distance. As we cross a road, a man nearly falls off his motorbike in sheer amazement. He struggles back upright, cursing.

We arrive at our venue for the evening, Clifford's Tower, the 13th century keep of York Castle. We climb the stone steps and step over rope barriers onto the grassy path around the tower itself, a National Trust restricted area. We form a circumference and begin singing an ancient rune-chant to awaken the magical energies of the city. We like the idea that the great Viking poet and sorcerer, Egil Skallagrimsson, imprisoned in York by its self-styled king Eric Bloodaxe, would have recognized our sung staves.

Time stretches out, so I don't know how long we're standing there singing, but at some point I look down into the streets below and see a crowd of smartly-dressed people coming out of a concert, turning their tourist cameras on us. Not only has no-one bothered us, but we've become the evening's main attraction.

On the way back, we stop off in a pub, order fourteen Glenlivets, shout 'Choyofaque!' and drink them down, to stares which mix puzzlement, amusement and mild hostility from the busy crowd. We congratulate ourselves at getting back to base safely.

A public working can bring out the magic of the most unlikely places. To spread magic over our home city, we generated a series of public rituals using the Chaotic technique of sticking a chopstick through a spinning map, eight times. Where each stab landed, we designed a ritual that fitted in with that place.

One of the locations was the local Mecca Casino, so we all got suited and booted in our lucky gear for a magical night out at the roulette tables. It turned out rather well; in the course of an evening's fun, doing something I'd never done before, I came out even, as did Soror S. and Frater M., while Soror L. was up to the tune of about £75.

Of course, there have also been one or two small disasters—a public invocation of Eris ended in a fistfight between one of our number and an old foe of his in the audience. That was a long time ago, and I think we've learned a few things since then.

ORIGINS

A sceptical, evidence-based approach to meditation, psychic powers and ritual magic; intense shamanistic-style rites and magical public performances; groups who work together for as long as they're brilliant, then dissolve to allow new, temporary autonomous combinations to form: where did this blend of influences come from?

We often trace core ideas in chaos magic back to Austin Spare's free-form sorcery, decades before Lionel Snell's *SSOTBME* or Peter Carroll's *Liber Null*, but the magicians who refined this approach grew up in 1950s and 60s Britain. This was a time when tradition had been consigned to the past, religion seemed to be dead or dying and the optimism of progress wasn't looking too healthy either.

Those who set out to explore the mysteries in that era found themselves short of useful models. On the right hand, there was the rehash of world-denying mysticism that trailed along after the psychedelic party of the 60s, and on the left, a magical scene which was in a rather bad way. A few decades before, the main influence would have been the work of Aleister Crowley, but by the late 1970s the main promoter of that current, the OTO, had abandoned the magical vanguard and seemed at pains to add to the Thelemic trinity of Life, Love and Liberty the even greater power of Litigation. To many a newcomer, the whole scene looked weary, a stultifying influence on the romance of the magical quest.

But it seems that magic is coded into our very DNA; this was a generation that found its own magical experiences and as a result uncovered a slew of uncharted weirdness to explain to itself. Energized by the DIY attitude that flowered briefly into Punk, a small number of people reinvented magic, based on their critical evaluation of personal experience.

The evidence-based approach is a robust one; it is much easier to be rigorous about checking the effects of sorcery when you're aiming for a visible effect in consensus reality. This enables chaos magicians to manage without a dogma to fall back on, but it also means that standards must be high, you can't fluff it.

Thirty years ago, chaos magic set the bar for standards of evidence, and, I think it's fair to say, has influenced most worthwhile magical organisations and currents in the direction of greater openness to ideas and greater rigour in practice and evaluation. There is in many cases a clear reason for this: most of the ancient magical traditions that we study are deficient in technical information—they tell you where to go, but not how to get there. If magic can be done using any belief system, then the basic, technical knowledge you gain from working the chaos approach can be applied to any traditional system you choose as your life's work. As a result of this, many of the major players in various areas of modern magic developed their practical magic in the IOT.

Chaos magic is well-suited to our era: it embraces scientific evidence and ideas but remains magical, not getting stuck in that one, narrow interpretation of experience. It does not demand that you relinquish your critical thinking and buy into some ready-made belief system, and so it provides for many the only possible jumping-off point from the common illusions of our age into the multiverse of magic.

The minimalism of the chaos approach is based on the two core ideas of 'Gnosis'—i.e. an extraordinary state of consciousness—and 'Belief-Shifting', the use of belief as a technique. There is little doubt that, on its own, changing a belief empowers your magic.

This formula can be summarized as Belief is Power and, whilst it's far from true that if you believe enough you can do anything (a New Age concept)—nonetheless, it has to be true that if you believe you can influence the world, you might, but if you don't, then you can't.

So: dare to disbelieve. And then—dare to believe! Choyofaque!

What Did Chaos Magic Ever Do For Me?

Soror Brigit

The world is not as it seems. You are more than you ever imagined you can be. You are less than you ever imagined you can be. I can hear you now, thinking 'But I already know this. Why is she giving me such platitudes?'

I thought I knew it too, but the knowledge lived only in my head. What the Pact did for me was to translate that knowing of the brain into the cells and molecules of my body. And do I know now that I am more, and less, than I ever imagined I could be? I have caught a glimpse of it, but having glimpsed it life will never look the same way again.

Now I know more completely that what I see during my daily life is only a fraction of what there is, and that what I see is illusionary, a distortion of the universe.

I joined the Pact for very simple reasons. Having done magick on my own for many years, I needed a group of peers to develop myself further. There are some areas of magick that are difficult to do on your own and would be dangerous to attempt. The Pact offered a group of experienced magicians who would enable me to progress in a safe way, where I would know that if anything happened I could not deal with then there would be plenty of people around who could help. I have found, during my five years in the

IOT, that this has been the case whenever I have needed a person to rely on, or any other form of help. More than that, I now feel that the magical development that has occurred has turned me into someone who can handle almost anything myself.

But why did I join the Pact and not some other magical group? Easy! This was the magical organisation that had a working a group in the city where I live—a very practical reason. I did not know back then that the Pact was to become such a significant part of my life. It's said that when the student is ready the teacher appears, but it was an IOT working group that appeared at the exact time I was ready to start working within a group. Coincidence? I don't think so!

While I joined the Pact largely because they were there, this is not the reason I have stayed for five years. What has kept me is the discovery of what I really am about, discovering skills and abilities that I never knew I had.

An experienced magician has told me on more than one occasion that the most important magical act an individual can perform is personal metamorphosis—using your magick to make positive changes to yourself and your life, and I have found that he was completely right in this. There is nothing more empowering than the discovery of self and non-self.

I have also been told by an experienced witch that you cannot come to know yourself unless you embrace your shadow side—that part of your being which you do not want to acknowledge; because it will throw everything you feel and think into disarray and confusion. Embracing a part of my shadow with the support of my peers completely changed my life. I no longer completely identify with the quiet, often retiring female that has often manifested as my personality. Now I know what lies beneath—all things and no things!

So I joined the Pact, as a novice, as a quiet and not very forthcoming individual who had always kept her magick secret, away from the eyes of others, into an organisation where the sharing of magical knowledge was actively encouraged. This was the first stage of my personal metamorphosis, turning this person who had never done a ritual in front of anyone into someone who felt confident and competent to do so. I embraced this as much as I was able, although the first time I performed a ritual in front of a number of people I'm sure my face turned a lovely shade of green because I felt like I wanted to throw up. But I did it—and you know what? It worked! The ritual was designed to cure someone of a brain tumour. The next time he went for a scan the tumour had shrunk and the medics could not say why. It later disappeared altogether and the individual is alive and well today. This made me think that if the Pact can do this, then this is a group I want to stay with! Encouraged by these successes I attended a gathering of magicians from all over the world. There I made the decision to volunteer for a type of magick I had never done before. Something that would expand my boundaries and challenge me and was something that I would most definitely not normally do. After all, I did not join the Pact because I wanted to keep on doing the same things. I was hungry for something different, something new, something else! I wanted something... but was not sure what that something was.

This was a ritual involving use of the scourge. Now, I had always thought of myself as 'not that kind of girl'. I have already mentioned that I was the shy and retiring type, so being skyclad and scourged in front of an audience presented me with a huge challenge. But it was a challenge that I was up for. This was different, this was new, this was something else.

As I felt the scourges find their mark, I sensed my energies changing, myself and my personality becoming smaller and smaller, until finally there was no me in the usual sense at all. And then something else emerged—a self I never knew I had. There was a wildness about it, an energy that scared me shitless, yet which also felt more real than any other sense I ever had of myself. And that's how it has been for me: if I'm not scared shitless at least some of the time I do magick, then I feel disappointed. I see the fear as a signal that I'm doing something real, something that blurs the image that I have of myself, something that stretches my ego beyond its comfort zone. In that moment I had broken what was a significant taboo for myself, and in doing so I found that I was more, bigger than myself. But to do that I had to lose the self, surrender to the scourge and lose my sense of self and ego. What could be more 'Thanateros' than that? Thanatos, as we know, is the god of death, and in this ritual my ego dissolved completely—I had a little death experience. Eros, the god of sex and life, woke me up to a new self and—yes—the sexual energy was very high as well!

After doing this ritual I could no longer believe in myself as someone who was quiet and retiring. That notion of the self no longer made sense, because if I have the confidence to do BDSM ritual, then how could I continue to believe in myself as a person with low confidence? From that moment a new self emerged; one that was more sociable, more confident, and with higher self-esteem.

Sometime after this experience I devised another ritual based on BDSM. The statement of my intent was to be able to speak effectively in public, as this was an area that I was finding difficult. As the scourge hit its mark I began to laugh—in that moment I found the whole concept of my being nervous of public speaking ridiculous. Given that I was skyclad and being scourged in front of a group of people, how could I possibly be afraid to talk to them? From that moment onwards speaking in public was no longer something that bothered me. I now speak before large groups on a regular basis.

Since working the BDSM paradigm I have felt an opening of awareness of the self, of what I really am. The rituals led to a questioning and a revaluation of self-belief. My inner deviant had awakened and, after years of suppression, it was ready to party. And so party it did.

It is through this type of magick that I have found the stillness, that quiet place within where there is no thought, where there is no you, and yet there is you.

In my BDSM rituals I am always the Sub. There is a reason for this: after experimenting with various roles I had decided that I am what is known as a 'switch', which means I can perform any role. However, my magical partner is definitely not a Sub and I could not bring myself to act the part of Dom if I knew my partner was not enjoying it. In every magical relationship within BDSM these roles need to be carefully thought out to prevent any magical mishap.

An important thing to think about when doing this type of magick is the reactions of others. When you talk about this magick with other practitioners, you need to be very careful to whom you talk. Some will view your interest in this type of magick as an excuse to behave badly towards you —for example, seeing you as sexual fair-game.

A really good Dom is a gentleman or gentlewoman who understands the needs of the Sub and will never try to coerce you into anything that you really do not want.

Finding one's sacred perversion is just that— sacred—and not to be laid bare to those who will use it for unintended means.

You need to choose your Dom with care because this type of magick is not about mindlessly hitting on another person. A Dom has to build up the magical space, be aware of the Sub's pain threshold, guide the Sub and hold the Sub's will. A really good Dom is always aware of the Sub's reactions during a ritual. Using the scourge or the paddle is something that takes practice. It is a real art to attain the smooth drumming motions on the Sub's body that pushes them further into trance. This trance state is known as 'subspace', a highly suggestible, and also highly vulnerable altered state of consciousness. In subspace I find that it really is impossible not to do what my Dom tells me, because I am in a very strong hypnotic trance. One time, my Dom bound my hands energetically, by placing my hands in position and telling me that my hands were bound and I could not move them unless he said so. And it really was impossible for me to move my hands from where he had positioned them until he told me. For these reasons choose your Dom with care. There needs to be a great deal of trust and respect within this magical partnership for both of you. The Sub needs to know that the Dom cares enough not to push them too far, and the Dom needs to know that the Sub won't go to the police or cry assault after the rite.

For anyone thinking, 'Great, I can put someone into trance and make them do what I want,'—it doesn't work that way. You cannot put someone into subspace unless they want to be there, so it's no good attempting to use this technique to manipulate anyone against their will.

Another issue to watch is how far you are prepared to go on being a Sub or Dom. For my part, the role of Sub exists only as long as the ritual. Outside the ritual scene, I'm anything but a Sub to my Dom. Most of the BDSM rituals we have performed, I have written them myself, so the Sub role exists for me only in a very specific context.

Nothing in my experience is more Thanateros than this, the pain of the scourge bringing in the death of the ego, and then Eros energy bringing in sex and life. This has led to an experience of Baphomet like no other I have ever had. I once used these BDSM techniques in a ritual to connect with Gaia-Malkuth-Baphomet, which was quite a ride. The bondage equipment connected me to the earth and was all designed to relate to the element of earth. The noise from the paddles acted as a drum, which literally beat me deeper and deeper into trance. I saw all sorts of visuals, as intense as any LSD trip I've ever been on. I saw the world teeming with life. Then I heard sounds, the sounds of birth and the sounds of death, which started like a heartbeat. This noise become faster and faster, until a whirring sound was all that I could hear. Nothing has ever connected me more strongly to the planet than this ritual. It changed me very deeply. I began to feel more compassion and this was reflected in changes to my lifestyle.

One of the most interesting pieces of magick I have done, with much assistance from a Dom, was the integration of BDSM into the Thanateros Rite as written by Peter Carroll. I worked with a different Dom during this ritual, which added an extra frisson. The Thanateros Rite was performed whilst the scourging took place. The sense of utter confusion arising from the BDSM process produced a gnosis that added energy to the Thanateros current. What I experienced was a deeper level of Thanateros than ever before. As my ego left, I floated gently into subspace and then found myself wakening back into life.

I have found the BDSM experience very spiritual, and I can see exactly why so many people from different religions have adopted these methods throughout history.

The spirituality of BDSM is something that is rarely written about. There are some publications on the market but not many. Up until this point, if I was interested in a piece of magick I could read what other people had done and follow their techniques and maybe come up with a few ideas of my own. With BDSM it was like a desert. There really was very little information around. Neither is this a central part of the magick of the IOT.

For these reasons I was forced to rely on my own creativity and to work within my own spirituality. Luckily there were people around me who, while they could not quite comprehend why I would be interested in magick that rendered physical pain, nonetheless supported me in my pursuit for self-discovery through pain and sex.

One thing about the IOT I want to mention here is that nothing is compulsory. There are a lot of different techniques and magical styles within the IOT. BDSM magick is one of my paradigms, but it is not shared by everyone. Also, in the IOT, if you do not like a paradigm then you can opt out of the ritual. Everything is permitted, including choosing not to participate in a ritual you don't agree with. What you will find in the IOT is support for your own journey of self-development, which takes everyone in their own individual direction. You can pursue your spirituality in any way that pleases you. I chose the BDSM way.

Working with deities within a BDSM context is a route I've explored in particular. After all, a devotee is—when all is said and done—a Sub to their god. Deities such as Kali and Inanna are very good to work with in this way.

The following ritual is an example of what can be done with BDSM. There are many different ways of achieving the same aim; this is only one of them.

KALI MA RITUAL

Kali is a goddess on the periphery of modern Hinduism. She is one of the goddesses of Tantra. It is possible she pre-existed Hinduism and her power was so strong that she could not be 'written out' as the new faith became dominant, and so she was integrated into the mainstream Hindu pantheon.

In Hinduism the ultimate figure is Brahman—the source, the energy from which the world was created. The first to be created from Brahman were Brahma, Vishnu and Shiva. Which one came first depends on which branch of Hinduism you follow. Followers of Shiva refer to Shiva as 'first born', followers of Brahma refer to Brahma as 'first born', so it really depends on one's point of view. Kali is often seen as the consort or daughter of Shiva.

In some traditions, however, Kali is seen as the spouse of Brahman or as the first-born. She is the mother who created all and to whom we all return when we die. It is she who creates the universe, and destroys the universe, and integrates all of the energies of Brahma the creator, Shiva the destroyer and Vishnu the Preserver. For this reason Kali is often portrayed as having many arms, each arm performing a specific function. The most common depiction of Kali represents her with four arms but other depictions show her with thousands upon thousands, symbolising her many functions and abilities in the order and chaos of the universe.

Her name means 'the black one' as she is the source of all things, she is the limitless void. Her name also means 'time'; the name 'Kali' comes from 'kala', meaning 'time'. In this way she is the all-devouring power of time.

Kali is often associated with overcoming the ego and with works of personal illumination in magick. In pictures, she is often seen wearing a necklace of severed heads. These can be interpreted as the heads of demons that, if they touch the ground, will destroy the world, and so Kali keeps us safe by keeping them around her neck. Another interpretation of this image (the one that I prefer) is that each of the severed heads represents a letter of the Sanskrit alphabet, and so Kali has 'decapitated words', because the experience of enlightenment takes us beyond words.

There are also many different ways of working with Kali. For example:

THE PATH OF THE DEVOTEE

This path involves working with Kali as a child goes to its mother, with devotion and surrender to the goddess.

THE PATH OF THE SAGE

This path involves meditating on the image of Kali and through this one finds enlightenment, through considering the teachings in the image.

THE PATH OF THE HERO

The hero boldly faces the challenges of liberation by acts of taboo-breaking and challenging their most cherished beliefs.

In the ritual I'm about to describe, we did all three things: we called for the mother and I surrendered to the scourge; I boldly went inside myself to find liberation; and we considered the imagery that Kali presents.

SOME INFORMATION ON TANTRA

There are a number of different Tantric paths, but in general Tantra involves liberation and union with deity by breaking taboos and cultural norms. The Tantric practitioner goes beyond the rules made up to control people, in order to experience liberation and the dissolution of the ego. Tantric yogis will often use techniques to modify the ego, allowing them to see beyond cultural conditioning.

Traditional Tantric practitioners undergo much training before embarking on any form of taboo-breaking. This may include breathing and meditation techniques. Taboo-breaking is an advanced technique, not to be embarked upon lightly. I would advise anyone to think about this very carefully before performing such a ritual.

THE RITUAL

The ritual works on four colours of magick:

YELLOW – Ego magick: the search for illumination and for moving a little out of one's comfort zones.

BLACK – The dissolution of something in one's life that prevents liberation.

OCTARINE – We are calling on a powerful goddess of magick.

GREEN – Each person in the ritual is helping the whole achieve their goals, whatever part they play, so if you were wielding the scourge, it is less about 'hitting a person' than helping yourself and your fellow magicians achieve their goals—as they are also helping you by receiving the scourge. The ritual also forms a devotion to Kali and should be performed in the spirit of green magick and devotion. The object is not to beat the crap out of someone, but to take someone to their edge so that they can enter a deep level of trance and charge-up the magick.

Each participant is to write down two sigils, one to represent an issue that they want to transcend—something that is hindering personal freedom and growth—and another to represent what you want instead, the liberation and freedom that you wish to experience.

STARTING THE RITUAL

Use a statement of intent that feels right to you, for example: 'I have experienced liberation through Kali.' *[Soror Brigit uses the technique of stating intents as if they have already happened, rather than as future desires. It seems to work for her fairly well! Ed.*]

Sit in a semicircle facing an image of Kali. Start by chanting Om three times. Then use any Kali chant you wish. It is important to do this part first as it sets the scene for the rest of the ritual. Use any Kali chant that is pleasing to you. Chant with much love and devotion.

As the energy of the chant builds, a number of ritual items are to be passed around the group to meditate upon, and consider how these represent the issue you want to be liberated from. These items can be:

COLLAR

This represents how the issue enslaves you, so that your will is not your own.

SHACKLES

It is better to use leather cuffs rather than metal handcuffs, as the latter can be very uncomfortable and can cause damage to the wrists or feet if closed too tightly. Leather cuffs are a lot softer on the skin and—more importantly—can be cut off with sharp scissors if the key is lost.

BLINDFOLD

This represents how your issue prevents you from seeing clearly.

ROPE

This can represent how the issue binds you and prevents freedom.

GAG

How the issue prevents you from expressing yourself in the world.

When these ritual items have been handled by everyone, a cauldron is passed around and the sigils, which represent what you no longer need, are placed into the cauldron and burned.

Items that represent liberation are now passed around for each person to mediate upon.

THE SCOURGE

This represents the element of air because it passes through the air, bringing the air-qualities of inspiration, clarity and freshness to help free you. The scourge also represents fire, because this is how it feels when it impacts on the skin, bringing the energy of creativity and inspiration.

THE PADDLE

This represents the element of water, supplying fluidity and flexibility and enabling one to move away from the undesired state to the one that you want to manifest. As the paddle impacts it provides the physical sensation of earth hitting the Sub with a thud, enabling the grounding of new energy into manifestation.

A space is set up in the middle of the room for the Sub and Dom. Everyone else stands in a circle around them. The sigils of what we want to manifest are placed in front of the Sub. The Dom places the bondage items on the Sub, stating clearly what each of them symbolises. The Dom should be skilled enough to take the Sub into trance before the scourging starts. It is essential for the Sub to be blindfolded as this enables them to travel more deeply into the other worlds to find the energy for charging the sigils.

Whilst the scourging is done the other participants move in a clockwise direction drumming and chanting the words 'Kali ma', whilst thinking about Kali and making enthused devotions.

When the Dom feels that the energy has built up enough, he or she removes the blindfold very quickly from the Sub so that the first thing she or he sees will be the sigils, which will then receive a very powerful charge.

The bondage gear is removed with statements from the Dom that we are now liberated and free. For example, 'Your shackles are removed from your hands, and you are now effective in the world.'

When the Sub has charged the sigils a sacrament of red wine is passed around and everyone drinks to Kali.

My experience of this ritual, as the Sub, was very intense. As soon as my very talented Dom put the collar around my neck, I entered into a deep subspace. My will was not my own; it was in the hands of the goddess, who spoke to me through my Dom as a priest of Kali. At this stage it would have been impossible not to do anything the Dom asked of me.

The ritual objects that I wore, coupled with the chanting, was very powerful. I could hear the chanting fading away and then there was nothing. A silence in which I was not aware of anything else going on in the room. Then I saw her: a large tiger emerging from the depths. I was able to take some of this energy and bring it back to charge the sigils that had been placed before me. As I focused on the sigils I could see the tiger in front of me, on the paper, moving around and within the sigils, giving them her energy.

So what did the Pact ever do for me? It took me on a journey of self-discovery during which I found that I was not who I thought I was. I was bigger than I ever imagined and less than I ever imagined. I found that my personality is only a small part of who I really am. Through working with my sacred perversion, I have found a greater tolerance for others, a greater love for others. People in glass houses really don't throw stones, so I became more accepting of other people's strange little ways. I found through connecting to Gaia during a BDSM rite a great love and respect for the earth that I did not have before, and made changes in my life because of that. I went from being someone who began her career in the Pact so nervous of presenting rituals that I felt physically sick to being someone who felt fully confident. And this confidence has impacted on every single area of my life.

The journey continues. I wonder where it will take me next?

NOTE:

BDSM magick can be very dangerous. Soror Brigit actively discourages inexperienced people from engaging in such activities and advises no one to attempt any of these rituals without receiving training in the specific techniques involved.

Liber Phurba
Frater Elijah

The Magicians who roll the magic dagger between their palms, who fling white mustard seed as a magic substance, who perform destructive magic with magic weapons: avert them! Turn back their strength upon them!

–A prayer to Tara from the scholar Vagisvarakirti, from the texts 'Cheating Death'.

This piece provides an understanding of what a phurba is, and its symbolism. I've also included a story-style example of a working with a phurba, to aid connection with it 'as one'.

I want to approach this in a malleable way, in terms of symbolism rather than focussing on vajrakilaya or the more static ideas associated with phurba practice. There are no health and safety assessments. This doesn't come with any warnings such as, 'This work can be extremely dangerous and should only be attempted if you are of sound body and mind.' Almost everything is dangerous, and a sound body and mind isn't necessarily much of a help with magick. The idea propagated by some fluffy new age types that a twat who drinks organic pro-biotic drinks, doesn't eat fatty foods, waves at the sun saying 'blessings be', who has a membership at an ethical gym and only enchants in a way that 'harms none' might be better able to perform more useful magick than some aging, diseased shaman in a freezing cave who has been gnawing on psilocybin for days but hasn't eaten a square meal in a week is clearly complete shit. It's always good to see that authors who preach lifestyle commandments, far from looking like a bronzed Adonis often have the waistline of a slave-trader and the hairline of Gail Porter.

A phurba is a magical dagger used for weather magic, killing demons, exorcism and healing. The history of the phurba is intermingled between traditions and obscured by the mists of time, but it is widely held that they are the mighty descendants of humble nails or tent pegs. Phurba, or 'kila' in Sanskrit, translates as 'nail', though there are other likely origins, such as shamanic drum-sticks and even three-sided epipaleolithic flints, which when attached to a handle look suspiciously like phurbas.

Nails and pegs have a history of magical use for two main purposes: consecrating or protecting important areas, and for tying — i.e. transferring negative forces from the afflicted into whatever the nail is hammered into. Nails have a long association with demons. For example, in India they are used to imprison demons in emetic nut trees. Phurbas can be found in an area stretching from South West Russia to Pakistan, down through Bhutan and Tibet and across to Japan. This large area of use and unique geography has meant there has been both a nourishing incubation of different traditions, as well as a rich cross-fertilisation of ideas, spread over time by travelling practitioners and nomadic peoples.

One thing that is certain is that phurba usage predates Buddhism, and often seems at odds with it, since phurbas are used for the killing of sentient demons. It is likely that dagger cults were so widespread that Buddhism had to incorporate aspects of them, in the same way that the early Christian church adopted pre-existing pagan ideas, festivals and themes to aid its integration.

Phurbas are heavy with the symbolism of three: three sections to the body, three blades, three parts to the handle and three faces of the deity. The phurba is the masculine Axis Mundi. It is the practitioner as well as the deity combined. As such, the phurba is also the form the practitioner takes when travelling astrally.

PHURBA, FROM TIP TO TAIL: BLADE!

The Phurba tip opens into a three-edged blade. The three edges are in turn blades themselves and cut through the three poisons: ignorance, desire and hatred. They control the past, the future and the right-now, and they look after the above, the below and the right-here.

Phurbas may have snakes and fire emblazoned on the knife faces, probably to aid (or as a consequence of) the phurba being visualised as radiating vajra fire and kundalini power. Wooden phurbas often have shamanic elements and calendar symbols, such as moons within suns, to represent their respective power.

The three-edged blade is held in place by the jaws of Makara (a cosmic crocodile-elephant-dolphin-thing) that can also represent Karkadhvaja, the God of lust. Makara has also been 'identified' as Trunko, the 'fish like a polar bear', which is said to have lost a fight with orcas of the coast of South Africa before drifting lifelessly ashore (as reported by The Daily Mail on October 25th, 1924). Think: ferocity, lust and certainty. (Although, admittedly, I wouldn't think of Trunko while contemplating these things.)

The blade symbolism then flows into the handle.

DORJE HANDLE!

A vajra, or dorje, is the thunderbolt, the sceptre, but more than this it is the diamond. Think of explosive energy that is indestructible. Indra was the original wielder of this thunderbolt sceptre; similar to an eastern Thor, but with the vajra as his hammer, if you like the northern tradition. Indra is the king of the gods, the god of storms and rainfall. Indra's Sceptre was taken by Buddha Shakuamuni, who hammered the dangerous spikes together as a sceptre of peace. What better housing for a ferocious, cosmic crocodile head and a three-sided demon-killing blade?

With a glance back to the blade, the snakes and Makra, it is also worth mentioning that Indra's most famous fight was with Vritra, the serpent who stole all the water from the earth. Indra smashed his Sceptre down on the snake's head to bring the water back. The vajra's position above the head of Makra and the Naga serpents could be a reference to this.

The vajra is a diamond of spiritual power. 'Vajra' in Sanskrit means 'diamond', and 'dorje' means 'the Lord of Stones' or 'diamond'.

The symbolism of the dorje is sort of a map of the expansion of the universe (or consciousness) in the shape of a diamond sceptre. The central point is the no-thing at the centre of existence. From that, in each direction, spring two lotus blossoms representing consciousness. From these emanates 'space', representing our three-dimensional world, surrounded by metal spokes symbolising enlightenment. These spokes then re-converge to a point of perennial monism. On the phurba, this point of monism also becomes the Eternal Knot—which can mean a shitload of things. I like the idea that it shows the dance of opposing forces in a dualistic world becoming the perfect union. Of the two knots, it is said that one holds Nirvana, and the other Samsara.

POMMEL!

After the knot is usually the three heads of the phurba deity: one peaceful, one joyful and one wrathful. The three heads represent Speech, Mind and Body—but don't forget that this is 'speech' in Tibetan Tantra: it comes in light and colours and can control the mundane as well as alter the spiritual. After the three heads, there is often a horse-head representing Tamdin, a centaur god of great power and husband to Marici, 'The Pig Face', who was also married to the awesome and bullish Yama. Tamdin is extremely wrathful and subdues beings that can't be tamed through peaceful means—and you'd need to be tough, to share a wife with Yama.

I live in the West and this is a description of the most common phurba symbolism I have seen, but it is by no means meant to be definitive. Blades can come with evocationary prayers, eagles attacking the snakes (the snakes representing the material and the earthbound, and the eagle representing the heavens and the divine). The handle can also have patterns, leaves and lotus, or be plain. In the place of Tamdin, pommels might depict snow leopards, eagles and many other animals. And it is not only animals—mushrooms are often used too. I'll let you draw your own conclusions why.

CREATION

To make a phurba, unless you are an expert in ironmongery, which I am not, it is probably easiest to make them from wood. I would suggest taking a saw or hatchet, performing a ritual to help you find your phurba, and heading off into the wilderness.

It's good to call upon the aid of the deity you will be harnessing with the phurba to aid you in the search. I have used Green Tara and Yama—not in their normal guises, but in ones that have become entwined in my psyche, in a similar style to the way that Eros and Thanatos are viewed in Peter Carroll's early works as the driving forces of human existence.

I think you will know when you have found your phurba. Do not worry too much about what type of wood to use, but look for a branch that doesn't have too many knots in it and looks straight enough for 'use'. The use will be rubbing it between your palms. Remember that it will become smaller as you carve it! You might find it useful to ask or repay the tree for the branch you take, if that feels natural to you. Cut it a bit longer than the length you want and start to roll it between your hands, eyes shut, meditating on your deity. Does it feel right? If so, you can start to carve. I used a box cutter or Stanley knife for the majority of the work, and a soft pencil for sketching out the parts I wanted to get rid of. The sketching really helps with getting the proportions right. Anoint it with blood, and any other bodily fluids that seem appropriate. What you are aiming for is you, the phurba and the deity as the same thing. I would suggest doing something similar to Reiki, or whatever else you feel will pass chi, la, or life-force between the phurba, you and the deity. It will probably be hard at first to lose the idea of duality. The story I'm about to tell concerns a ritual I used to dissolve it. Are you sitting comfortably?

THEN I'LL BEGIN

In the dark, under the forest's malignant canopy, I trudged, a hunched figure, almost silent in my trespass. The screech of an owl cut through the night sky as I approached the side of a halcyon lake.

Entering the boundary walls of a strange folly, I was enveloped by a fleeting injection of ice-cold intoxication, the hairs standing up on my arms, the temperature suddenly loose and errant. Navigating through the broken stones by torchlight, I entered a pitch- black corridor. The owl screeched again and a fox's howl ripped its reply across the valley.

The corridor widened and the entrance to a man-made chamber confronted me. (Made for magick? Made for sadness? Made for nothing?) The central chamber soon had a fire in its centre, its natural knee-height altar was then decorated with a Tara Tangka, a black and a white candle, incense, water, a kapala, a phurba and some mead with blood and red food-colouring added. A Gnostic Pentagram Ritual was performed using the phurba and then some of the mead was drunk from the kapala, the rest 'sprayed' around the chamber to represent blood.

The phurba held in front of me, dakinis visualised all around, the statement of intent was shouted: It is our will to become phurba now! White mustard seeds were thrown on the fire, offered to Agni. As the fire crackled I held the phurba between my palms and rubbed it back and forth in front of my solar plexus, the blade pointing to the floor. I felt a deep, relaxed concentration. As the phurba span I entered glossolalia until I found the mantra sung by the phurba, which then morphed into a (phonetic) Green Tara mantra: 'oaaammm tara, tu-tarre, tooo-ray, svoo haa.' This was vibrated over a period of about forty minutes to an hour (maybe more; time had become exceedingly slippery). While intoning, the phurba (still being rubbed between my palms) was slowly raised, until the culmination point of its rising above my head, no difference between it and me. It was a part of me, and I part of it. From this stabbing position phurba flew into the ground, unifying and spreading its unification throughout reality.

The cave was furious with static. I retired, as phurba, as Tara and as me to a smaller cavern with benches cut into the walls. I held the phurba and took a deep hit of DMT from a small pipe. Falling back against the stone wall, I was one being with Tara, with the phurba, my throat collapsing, my cheekbones retreating into his face, my torso melted into the ground, which gladly accepted me. From the depths I had come, and to the depths I was returning. A slow, forceful humming, deep, vibrating. Green nebulous gas twisting, surrounding, female, damp, dry, electric, erotic and sensual. Forcing, burrowing and flowing into the depth of pre-existence. Radiating information.

Later, time became slippery once more.

The corner of my mouth lifted and so did my body. A smile overcame my face, and there was a stillness at the core of my being.

Meht nopu htgnerts rieht kcab nrut! Meht treva! Snopaew cigam htiw cigam evitcurtsed mrofrep ohw, ecnatsbus cigam a sa dees dratsum etihw gnilfohw, smlap rieht neewteb reggad cigam eht llor ohw snaicigam eht.

—A prayer to Tara, from the scholar Vagisvarakirti (re-versed).

BIBLIOGRAPHY

Stephen Bayer, *The Cult of Tara: Magic and Ritual in Tibet* (Berkeley, CA: University of California Press, 1978).

Alexandra David-Neel, *Magic and Mystery in Tibet* (Harmondsworth: Penguin, 1971).

David Gordon White, *Tantra in Practice* (Princeton, NJ: Princeton University Press, 2000).

Lama Anagarika Govinda, *Foundations of Tibetan Mysticism* (York Beach, ME: Red Wheel Weiser, 1969).

Vessantara, *The Vajra and Bell* (Cambridge: Windhorse, 2004).

Thomas Marcotty, Dagger Blessing: The Tibetan Phurpa Cult: Reflections and Materials (New Delhi: D.K. Printworld, 1987).

Peter Carroll, *Liber Null & Psychonaut* (York Beach, ME: Weiser, 1987).

Magic in the Age of Reason

Frater Noctaris

This essay looks at magic and reality. Describes what it might be, how it might work and provides some nice examples of magic in action. Before that I will waffle on a bit about the scientific paradigm, its wonders and limitations.

Firstly, let's orientate ourselves in time and space. How, in this modern age, the age of information, the epoch of the Anthropocene, can any rational modern human believe in such an outlandish fancy as "the occult" or magic? How could any sensible person consider it anything other than bizarre and primitive outdated superstition?

There are as many explanations of magic as there are flavours and practitioners of it. I doubt any mage has the exact same idea of what it is. Unlike say, for example science, where everyone operates to the same simple rules and in terms of "Results" uses the exact same methodology. Conclusions on results are however prone to interpretation. But, science has a universal appeal; we know it works because it delivers us technology, atom bombs, relativity and quantum mechanics. It has also spawned failed philosophical interpretations, like Richard Dawkins and his so called God Delusion. If you want to see a clear example of "Science gone awry" then look no further than Dawkins and his troop of blind watchmaker materialists.

Science was never intended to be a philosophy; it is simply a way of doing things. Science, coupled with human ingenuity, has indeed yielded the most remarkable products, wonderful and dangerous. Looking to science for answers regarding meaning, purpose, subjective experience is futile, since it is not designed to nor can it ever provide us with explanations regarding our subjective self. It sounds obvious, but science can only answer scientific questions, and the subjective world is not in any way whatsoever, scientific.

Leaps and bounds made in neurobiology have shown that this or that part of brain lights up in synchrony with another part of the brain when such and such experience is being processed, biochemistry has shown that enzyme A rises as depression kicks in, or Hormone B rises as we fall in Love, it's even revealed changes in genetic expression with the recent internet Ice Bucket challenge, but this does not in any way provide a satisfactory explanation of any subjective experience. How do different bits of the brain, firing in synchrony across its cortex give rise to a singular experience? Say for example, the experience of the smell of a rose, close your eyes, block your ears, and smell the rose... the complex odour molecules bind to the receptors of the nose, with quantum precision, in a particular order, convert to electrical digitised nerve impulses, and 'somehow' give rise to the singular insular sensation. Same with hearing, hit a string at resonance, the vibrations at so many hertz hit the eardrum, and inside the ear your set of tuning forks are all exposed to the frequency, the biological tuning fork (made of hair) closest to that frequency falls into sympathetic harmonic resonance and 'somehow' presents us with the subjective experience of the sound. Science has no ability to explain this subjectivity; it is however remarkably excellent at explaining the mechanisms leading up to it. So what I'm trying to say here is let's not get scared of science, by its overpowering results upon us, nor the unreasonable effectiveness of mathematics as a descriptor of physical laws, instead let's understand science and in doing so be clear about its limitations in providing explanations in the subjective realms.

So when trying to use science to provide answers regarding big questions, it gives us, childish almost autistic responses.

"Where did the universe come from" ... It came from nowhere at all, for no reason in a single instant a space-time explosion from a naked singularity, and then everything happened by randomness and over time, energy became matter, matter became biology and biology became conscious all by itself totally by accident.

That is the best it's got to offer. And as the late Terence McKenna pointed, "Notice this is the limit case for credulity, if you can believe that, you can believe anything".

Now we understand that what we recently assumed to be "The Universe", that space containing all the galaxies which the Hubble space telescope reveals to us in the most astonishing clarity, we realise by peeking back in time into an accelerating expanding sphere about 14 billion light years in diameter that this galaxy-filled space may not be the totality of reality, but we are glimpsing suggestions that it may instead be a tiny short lived vacuole in a much, much, larger hyper-dimensional structure termed " The Bulk".

This universe didn't just start from nothing at all. That is obviously preposterous, this universe manifested because there are other pre-processes occurring in the bulk, it is perhaps the result of the formation of a black hole in a higher dimension. I can't tell you what the trigger was, but I can tell you, for sure, that prior to our local space-time vacuole, there was and is already an infinity of other stuff happening, an infinity of infinite variables in all parallels and all dimensions. I will also tell you something else that is a bit weird about our visible universe at its largest scales, hyper clusters of superclusters of galaxies form strands and networks, that poetically, as above so below, look very, very similar to microscopic samples of brain slices. Now, I obviously can't speculate on that phenomenon, but, in biology, form is function, and function is form, they are one and the same. The valid critique here is obviously that the images spanning countless millions of light years revealing filament networks of galactic hyper-clusters looking "like" a brain is cosmology, made of galaxies, not biology made of living material. Well, I ask rhetorically, how many stages down do you need to go in biology before it falls apart again back into ordinary non-animate matter; take a skin cell, pinch out a subcellular component, is that alive...? More simply I'm saying, if the universe looks like a brain, then it's probably doing brain stuff. Once on this track of fancy I can confabulate with confidence and state with wanton abandonment that the universe is processing information and thinking things into existence. I am at liberty to speculate that much. Whether or not you agree with me, you must admit that the recently discovered inter relations between reality and consciousness do suggest that consciousness is embedded into the space time manifold and material reality in a very deeply mysterious manner.

What I am feeling is that in some way, the universe is itself a living object. And that it's a living object as a tiny sub-component of a bulk. I'd suggest that the bulk is a good candidate for God, and since I am choosing to believe that I am A Chaos Magician, I choose to call this entirety, infinity of infinites, Baphomet.

An interesting side point, the brain is at present considered to be a computer by many. In times gone by it has been variously considered to be made of vapours, later as fluids, in the industrial revolution, thought was considered to be created in the brain by the actions of tiny machines, then in the 1960s it was described as a telephone exchange. What's happened here is that mankind seems to always equate the brain and its workings with his most up to date advanced technologies.

As a scientist, during my formative training, I became a materialist, and followed the dogma of Richard Dawkins with his so-called "God Delusion", my mindset became that of a scientist. I may very well have stayed in that paradigm, but, my doors of perception were blown off their hinges with the mindful use of psychedelics. I must add however, the most profound magical experiences that I've had have come directly from the world without the use of any drugs. In a moment I will narrate to you a set of events that I experienced. I don't know if you will agree with me, but I am now pretty sure that the world as described by modern science, the most advanced model that we have, falls pathetically short of a comprehensive descriptor, and instead we should perhaps cease reliance on science to provide anything other than a set of tools by which to measure our world. Science was never meant to be a philosophy, nor was it meant to provide anything other than prediction from repeatable results. Some of the latest findings at the edge of quantum mechanics suggest that we may be near the end of the scientific paradigm and hint at the beginning of a new discipline, for which at present we don't have a name.

The first "big" question, is how come there is (i) time and space and (ii) any matter/energy/information or anything at all here, where did it come from. Second to this is how come the particulate matter that makes our cosmos can end up as living creatures, and further, how come it can become conscious. How consciousness is related to reality is a deeper question.

The best take I've seen on this to date is The Cognitive-Theoretic Model of The Universe (CTMU, pronounced Cat Mew) by Christopher Langan, a nightclub bouncer, who happens to hold the highest IQ in the world. CTMU essentially states, the world is made of atoms, atoms subatomic particles, and if we continue this reduction eventually we reach a condition where only information remains, and the universe and its laws is a construct of the shimmering of this information matrix and the mathematical relationship between them. I'd urge you to have a look at CTMU, especially the bit where God pops out of his equations as an inevitable conclusion of the presence of the universe in the first place.

So magic, as Crowley describes it, "the Science and Art of causing Change to occur in conformity with Will". Well, that will do for me, I'm happy with that. The *reason* that I am a magician is because I have experienced magic. It's really that simple.

SYNCHRONICITY

This word is often misunderstood, as the layering of coincidences on coincidence. It is not. The term synchronicity was coined by C. Jung to explain the subjective experience of the unfolding of events in spacetime. This runs contrary to the scientific explanation of causality. We know that causality is true in all classical physics, but it does fail at the edges of quantum mechanics, where it has been shown unequivocally that the future can interfere with and influence the past. The magician often asks, what the future and the past are made of. What Jung was saying is that the unfolding of events can be given validity by the "meaning", the subjective experience of the unfolding of events. Like you think of someone, and they call you on the phone whilst you are thinking of them. You suspect that you are going to find a five pound note at a bus stop, and you do find one. Here we are beginning to enter the realm of magic, and leave the domino-like causality of science behind, letting it run its business of keeping the universe in place, whilst we as conscious autonomous magical entities are free to play in the field of The Lord.

I will give you an example of Synchronicity. When I tell people that I had telepathic communication with a tree, they often dismiss me as bit nuts, but when I recount the story, right at the end, they go pale and shit themselves.... Are you sitting comfortably?

One night in autumn I was sitting in my chair, looking out of the window of my flat on the top floor of a Victorian house, in Liverpool. The house was on top of a hill. My view was clear to the horizon, the Welsh Mountains in the distance, all across the city, over the River Mersey, onto the Wirral and fading towards Wales. In the night time, this view was made mainly of the swathes of orange sodium street lights that define modern Britain, hundreds, perhaps thousands of orange dots as far as the eye could see. However, the object that dominated my view was a 100-year-old magnificent Willow tree, majestic and strong, her branches leafless, about 20 foot directly in front of my window. My view was occluded by her plethora of branches. I could of course see through the tree, since it was free from leaves; in the summer, all I would have seen is the beautiful tree. So, looking towards Wales with no particular thing in mind, sitting there in neutral if you like, the gentle breeze passing through the branches makes them undulate in a random manner. As the branches move and sway gently, they temporarily occlude a street light or block of street lights and then reveal them again, so I get a kind of 'twinkling' effect from the breeze derived motion of the smallest branches of the tree. It was quite soporific, and by degrees, I became immersed in this, with no clear start point, I found myself immersed in a silent movie, a movie that showed the utter folly of mankind in his relentless assaults on the world's forests, the Armageddon-like consequence of unabated deforestation and some other stuff about the nature of interdependency of living systems. Enthralled, five or so minutes passed before I snapped out of my trance. Humorously, half joking, I said to my Woman, "I have just had telepathic contact with that Willow tree", and recounted the movie I'd just seen. She shrugged her shoulders dismissively and suggested I lay off the Skunk, a tiny bit hostile. In the morning I was sitting at my window, looking out towards Wales, puffing on my spliff, she touched me and clutched my shoulder, her face ashen, wide eyed, voice trembling. "Where is the Willow?" she asked…. I'd been sitting there and not even noticed the missing 100-year-old willow tree that the council had come to cut down that very morning.

So is this meaningful? Whether or not I had 'real' telepathic communication with a tree or not is irrelevant, it is the order of the unfolding of the events that is certainly and obviously meaningful at least to me. I have an unmistakable subjective experience involving the tree, the thrust of that experience is the stupidity of cutting down trees, and within the next twelve hours it's been cut down and destroyed. This is a clear example of a Jungian synchronicity in action. This too is the delicate nature of the experience of magic, how do we 'choose' to view our world? Here I find it quite difficult to remain totally rational regarding the experience. To me, it 'seems like' the tree was communicating with me.

Take a few magic mushrooms, and the whole forest will communicate, unambiguous, organic network of hypermorphing biological nature, dismantling of causality, amplification of and melding of intelligences with your own, temporary dissolution of subject and object, immersion into the oneness of the hypermind. But I could not possibly recommend this approach.

Whilst I am on the subject of High Weirdness happening to me, I may as well continue. I will start with my accidental self-initiated introduction to the occult. [*I'd like to point out this experience—and several others recounted here—occurred long before Frater Noctaris joined the IOT. Ed.*]

One night, I found myself as a backseat passenger in a stolen car full of recently stolen drugs and money and weapons. We ended up, in hiding, in a car park halfway up a Welsh mountain. Happy with a day's work well done, I ate just one of the tablets, it had an artsy logo printed on the front of it, I think it was MDMA. At first the gentle buzz was quite pleasing, then it became intense, and eventually, as it is supposed to, the reversal of my serotonin pumps, made me feel empathic ecstatic sensations, not to the people I was with but interestingly enough to the mountainous surroundings outside the car. After a spliff of the white widow skunk the visions began. It seemed to go beyond the ecstatic, and started to shimmer with suggestions of the mystical instead. I was unfamiliar with this type of intensity of experience. To say it was pleasant would be an understatement. The hallucinations started with the finger smudges on the windows and patterns of condensation being overlaid onto the rocks outside the car. At once I could see the smudges, and yet, paradoxically, I could clearly see the creature that they made sitting on a rock, looking away across the mountains. Like some kind of Goblin, it had an intricate set of patterns of light flying round its head, it was transparent, it was there clear as day and at the same time, I knew it was "just the drugs...". Over a few moments the transparency was lost and it became solid in form, the lights around its head becoming brighter and more intricate. The moment it turned its head and looked directly into me was overwhelming and rather disconcerting. Its blazing eyes hypnotised me, sucked me in, I was lost from this world, no longer in the back seat of a motor car. Instead, I found myself in a dimly lit natural rock tunnel, quite small, man sized. I felt like I was gliding or on skates rather than actually walking. In the distance, I could see the quintessential light at the end of the tunnel, just a flickering glow, so I continued towards it. As I got closer to the light, straining to see it, I became aware of some details, astonishing details. Once close enough to resolve fully, I saw the end of the tunnel was guarded by two serpent-like intertwined muscular giant pythons, so obviously Caduceus but at the time I was ignorant to this. As I got closer, the serpents kind of acknowledged me, and began the unlocking process; they untwined and unpaired from each other and stood guard now as individual pillars, one to my left and one to my right. In front of me was a precipice, a precipice of infinity. What was remarkable about it, looking into this void was that the entirety of it was constructed out of precious gems, rubies, emeralds, sapphires the size of tangerines, diamonds the size of asteroids. No single place in this void, no individual point contained anything other than infinite wealth, the whole part of it endless infinity of infinity on endless immeasurable wealth. Its beauty was astonishing, and I was utterly overwhelmed.

"But what does it mean?" I blurted out...

The reply... (like a Charlton Heston God, with reverb) "Crystal minerals do not hold intrinsic wealth, this is something your species invents, this is a picture of something to help you understand."

"Understand what?" I thought.

"The nature of wealth, its intrinsic value, its origin, and its source", came the instant reply.

"Is this is the aspect of the mind, locked behind the serpent guardians!" I asked.

"Yes..." it reverbed... "go on..."

"This is all within myself, therefore all wealth is intrinsically internal, and thus the keys to liberation already reside within me..."

"And your response to this revelation?" asked the overvoice.

"I must change my life, I must study neurochemistry, attempt to fathom the links between consciousness and reality and the nature of the subconscious."

"Bingo", said god, who promptly vanished, taking his pretty hallucinations with him.

Abruptly, I found myself back in the car, the goblin still shimmering into the background, the air thick with skunk smoke... I told my scally mates that I was no longer the person I just was, and instead was reborn, they laughed, oh how they laughed.

I was enrolled on a Biomedical Science degree three months later as a direct result of this experience and some fancy eloquence written in lieu of any formal A-level qualifications. I got some intertwined serpents tattooed on my arm as well, the tattoo artist got the image from a book by some bloke called Crowley, so, I read that book.

Let me tell you another story of high weirdness.

One winter's night, freezing cold and utterly still, I think I was about 18 years old; I went out to the yard to the outside tap to water the Great Danes. Holding

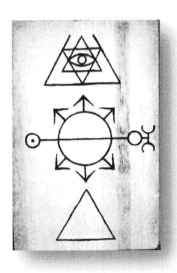

the bucket, I hear a deep powerful whooshing sound, like the sound a fire juggler's stick makes, deep not harsh, and overhead, just higher than the rooftops a bright blue ball of energy sped off leaving a persistence of vision tail behind it. It was the fastest thing I'd ever seen, and it was gone in less than half a second. The intensity of its presence more than making up for the brevity of its presence! The only way I can describe it, is like a macrocosmic electron, about fifty times the size of a football, the colour of an arc welding flame, high intense bright blue. "Ball Lightning" I hear you say... perhaps. But listen on... and consider there was not a single cloud in the sky.

The next day, my mate who lived in the rooftop caretaker's flat of the girls' school quarter mile from my house (my subsequent living in the art block of the sixth form girls' college is another story) came to me, and was excited about a weird light he'd seen rushing over the landscape. A quick discussion confirmed he had seen the same thing as I had, but to him, further away and higher up, he saw it for longer than I did, for about a second, but he described it as a silver-white horizontally squished ovoid, with a sharp lingering tail. Whenever I got high after this, my mind would always fixate on it, pondering its nature. Now, some thirty full years later, I still wonder; it forms a small but subjectively important part of a network of synchronous that were about to unfold over the next decade.

Having turned my back on a life of crime, and the handy cash it provided, I'd opted for a life dedicated to study after my meeting with the pythons' gallery of infinite wonder. My university grants were threadbare, my neglected grow room had been busted, so, I became a driver of taxis, black ones, hackney cabs... "where to guv?", that kind of thing. I did this in the night time, after university had finished. If I plugged 60 hours of driving, after the extortionate rental fee, it provided a modest income, enough for rent and food. If I didn't do 60 hours then I may as well not bother as the first 40 hours only covered the costs, and if I didn't do any hours then massive scary debt mounted up really fast. The sacrifice was that in my entire time at university never ever did I ever go out on the piss with the other students, and being a bit older than them, never really gelled properly in my group. I was always knackered, and often fell asleep during my lectures; I was not a model student by any means. Still, with the assistance of my newly discovered pharmaceutical branch of nootropics, hydergine, centrophenoxine, piracetam, and such, study became a doddle and I was top of the class. So top of the class in fact, they let me do an independent research topic rather than one of the honours projects on offer... I did electricity and fungal morphogeneis, best in the year...

Anyway, one night, just another boring dull taxi shift over, about 03:00am, I stopped outside of one of my girl friends' houses, on the sniff for a fuck, some supper and a bed for the night. This was Veronica, a brummie from the Black Country, living in Liverpool, working as a fitness trainer in a gym.

So, here I am, taxi shit over, in her garden, trying to throw pebbles at her top floor bedsit to wake her up. As I bent down to pick up another pebble... "it" started. Almost imperceptible, at first, mild, slow and gentle, a band of sensation progressed from my feet, up to my head, by the time I'd stood up straight, the sensation began again, but this time, a bit stronger and a bit faster, but still only just at the threshold of noticing, then again, a pulsation of sensation in a tightly constrained band, like how a scanner scans a document, now making itself clearly felt, moving upwards from the floor, into my feet and up through legs and torso to my head. Each time the process would repeat, it increased exponentially in intensity and the speed it traversed my body. Each pulse stronger and faster than the last. To explain what it felt like is impossible, but, I am familiar with the entirety of the range of physical sensations that my nervous system is capable of from agony to ecstasy, yet this sensation was entirely utterly different to anything within that scale range. An outlier, I was not aware my nervous system could transduce this kind of feeling, utterly alien, beyond nirvana, pleasure beyond pleasure, Samadhi, sex with god. Every orgasm you ever had rolled into one, does not even begin to describe it. Not sexual, not anything, just pure unadulterated alien god like transmission. And it was still happening, the pulses becoming so rapid that it moved from a digital experience to analogue, a continuous flow of starseed transmission no longer capable of increasing in speed, now just increasing in intensity. I screwed up my face, clenched my jaw, buttocks tightened, fists clenched, this overwhelming magnificence getting stronger and stronger, my arms moved naturally to cross over my chest, my hands now so tightly clenched they would have been white knuckling, still, the intensity increased...no longer able to remain clenched, I let out a "ahhhhhh" sound, opened my arms up to the sky at the same time as opening my eyes... And... there "it" was... an object in the sky, white undulating plasma, flickering, looking exactly like the white side of the Yin Yang symbol, but stretched out in a straight line, circular at the front with a sharp tapering tail and a massive black hole at its front. Flat against the sky, in 2D only, like a cartoon, it dropped out of the sky and vanished behind a block of flats. I was astonished, dumbfounded, and I was there in the garden just holding my pebble. After some time, I threw it at the window, woke her up, her big gleaming grin and sapphire blue eyes so beautiful. "Heelaw", she said to me in her thick Brummie accent... I didn't mention anything about this to her, there was no point, what could I possibly say that she would understand? Later that night she woke me. Shaking me violently, repeating over and over, "It's very very weird, very very strange... wake up, wake up...!". What had happened was that in the night, she'd opened her eyes, half awake, and in her own words, been confronted by an electric blue see-through clockwise spiral on my back, bright, and as soon as she thought, "what's that?" it disappeared, but left a funny feeling... It's of course impossible to divorce this from the mega event of the earlier evening, but I have no explanation whatsoever to offer. To this day the event with the "sensation" remains by far the single most astonishing and remarkable event of my life.

MAGIC IS ABOUT FREEDOM FROM BELIEF.

Some beliefs and some ideas, are contagious. Contagious like a virus. Examples of this are certain political dogma, and some religious systems. Islam is a good example, but so too is Communism. "I believe I'm a [Muslim][Christian][Communist]" these types of infection have some things in common. Firstly, they change the behavioural responses of the victim, and inherent in the package is the necessity to spread said package, in some cases, making it vital to either convert virgin, non-infected minds, or if conversion to said belief structure is not possible then to delete that mind from existing by killing it. This "type" of belief, very deeply ingrained controlling and with the need to spread resides in a subroutine of the brain located in the medial frontal cortex. So if your God or your Politics resides here, in this locus of the brain, then you're infected with a mind virus, or meme. It controls nearly every aspect of your personality from this location. Infected individuals will ignore reason and constructive argument, having to accept the booby prize of blind belief over rational argument. This can lead to all sorts of conflict, see these infected are not neutral, they are active in attempting to spread the meme, and can become lethally violent if individuals or groups refuse to take on the script. Communism only works if it takes over the world, and thus China and Russia after taking on the Marxist scripts, murdered between them 100,000,000 of their own people who refused or were not able to become the ideal vessel for the new ideas. Godless communism, versus the Bible belt fire and brimstone capitalism of the United States took mankind to the very very edge of complete man-made Armageddon. Perhaps only the more powerful overriding biological survival instincts saved us from ourselves in this case. But plainly it was an ideological clash, a belief battle that took us most recently to the brink of extinction

Magic, specifically my chosen flavour of chaos magic, has at its core, the knowledge of the power of belief and of meta belief. Through various ritual techniques it demonstrates the effectiveness of belief shifting, the conscious choice to *choose to believe* that something is true, for a bit, then dropping that system in favour of a new belief. Of course it's almost impossible to convince yourself of something being true when you know it's not. So we choose things that "could be" or "might be" true. For example, I would read some books on how the universe is a computer simulation, and once sufficiently enthused with the ideas of other thinkers, I would choose to believe that the universe was indeed a simulation, and once I'd done this, everywhere I looked I could find clear "evidence" that it was so. The inverse square law, the wave particle duality, the nature of information … everywhere I found proof that I was a Neo Matrix-like character in a sim. Later on, I dropped that belief in favour of a more complex one. But it is not the current model that one holds that is important, it is the position in the brain of the belief, "if" it resides in the medial frontal cortex, then it is in charge of the user rather than the user being in charge of it. Shifting beliefs ritually is a liberating experience and being free from any form of suppressive dogma is a vital skill for anyone who wishes to retain any degree of autonomy in a world mostly controlled by political dogma or religious ideals.

Whilst talking about politics I can only point out one very obvious observation, all current mainstream political ideology is a dichotomy essentially between left or right wing variants. Where the left has taken hold and allowed to run its course unabated (for example modern China with 70 years of unchallenged hard core communism) or where the right has taken hold (e.g., Modern America) both systems lead to the same place, following different routes. The left screams "cooperation comrades", the right screams you are free, work harder, watch these adverts, pay your taxes... Both systems when unchallenged give rise to the oligarchic classes and militarised police states and disempowerment of citizens. Just a few shadowy puppet masters owning 99% of everything, and leaving the remaining 1% available for everyone else to fight over. 1,000 people own 99% of the wealth on earth. Surely, this is screaming for a reset. Democracy or Communism or religion of any flavour are all distractions. The magician is free from them all. Belief to the magician is a tool, and he keeps it sharp and in good order.

THE MAGICIAN AND HIS WILLPOWER

The crux of a mage is his ability to change reality according to his will. Sure enough, science has validated that under certain conditions the observer, with his willpower, can change and influence random chaotic systems, that is everyone can do it, and it's a built-in function of the universe. The difference is that magician knows this, exploits it and practices it.

Some go so far as to say that the measure of a mage is how far from the mean can he shift the line. Have we got free will? Is the universe predetermined or is the future up for grabs? Well, personally I doubt that absolute free will can run unencumbered on a biological substrate brimming with instinctual commands. I think pragmatism is the key here, and we can say that we have freedom of choice within tightly constrained boundaries. So for example, you come to the fork in the road, and you can choose to go left or right, that is within bounds, but you can't choose to go off road or to go backwards. I'm not sure about the universe being predetermined or not, there are convincing arguments on both sides of that fence. Perhaps it's not as simple or as straightforward a dichotomy of it is, or it is not; it might be a blend of various parameters. The phenomenological formality of the occurrence of an event is probably not something we can actually get our heads around, fully.

I had an insight into free will one time. I was in Mexico at the Mayan temples in 1999, attending a drug conference. All the big names were there, Terence McKenna, Shulgin, the guy who discovered Viagra, and the some of the best drug dealers and clandestine chemists in the world. The drugs were... astonishingly strong and pure. Three things that were in great abundance were the local magic mushrooms and weed, actively peddled by the natives, and orange waxy DMT derived from Psychotria viridis; this combined with the availability of the entirety of *Pikhal* and *Tikhal* made for a heady combination.

I was already off my face on some kind of 2C-T-7 & 2C-B bromo dragonfly cocktail when they said we were going for a trek through the rainforest to the Temples. I followed, my short term memory wiped out like a 10 second goldfish, on a tiny loop of neurotoxic nirvana. I was already hallucinating wildly when we reached the temples, I think the microdot had kicked in by then, too. We climbed up the massive square steps to the door of the sacred and ancient pyramid structures. Once inside, we sat down on the stone seats, and it was all very mysterious and scary and of course, my paranoia kicked in, and I was worried they were going to sacrifice me. I clammed up a bit. The DMT pipe was loaded, packed to the rafters with the orange waxy DMT, legendary material, leaps and bounds more depthy than the current crop of Mimosa hostilis extract than any kitchen chemist can make these days. I was reluctant to smoke it, knowing full well what would happen from previous exposures. After the second lungful, I heard the characteristic pitch-increasing sound wave, and held the pipe away for someone to take off me. At that moment, my friend, Mr. Sky, leaned his jester head from outside the temple and simply said to "Smoke more", so I did, with the sine wave pitch already at uncomfortable volumes, and the pixilation already beginning to disintegrate my vision, I inhaled a third, then fourth lung full and in an instant I was gone.

My consciousness awareness was enveloped in blackness. The blackness was made of interlocking acute triangles, which were shimmering into and out of existence. I was greeted with a line of identical circus showmen turtles, on two legs, wearing top hats and holding black and white sticks, they started dancing doing the Cha, cha, cha and spinning the sticks like majorettes. There was a dark vaguely dystopian carnival vibe to it, and I was not impressed. I remember saying something like "no, I'm not having this shit" and suddenly it stopped. Then I remember being awestruck by the realisation that I had some modicum of control about what was happening to me, it felt a bit like a lucid dream. After some light speed tunnelling, I eventually reached the dome. I'd been here previously, a spherical space made of impossibly complex psychedelia and I was complete with 360° vision. Bright and stark, sharp angular morphing, this was the peak of all my previous DMT trips and the reason I'd stopped taking it. Because for all its beauty there is a sensation of insanity around it, like it's something you're not really supposed to be looking at, and once seen, not worth the risk of repeating since it is utterly totally devoid of any meaning whatsoever. However this time, I was lucid, and not lost in astonishment. The familiarity of it allowed me to take a deep breath, a moment of introspection was all it took, and I had the ability to formulate a question. I asked myself, "Why am I so encumbered with self-destructive habits like nicotine smoking and internet pornography, why do I keep repeating these actions even after I decide I no longer choose to engage in them?". One of the outer rims of the DMT sphere opened up, and flipped open. There was a mythic giant god form, like a statue from Jason and the Argonauts, or a dead ringer for the Goddess from the Crowley deck. In terms of size I was about halfway up its big toe. I was standing at its feet; it had really corny cheap sci-fi laser beams emanating from its third eye and a halo with like a notice board of glyphs moving on it. At this point nothing seemed weird, or out of the ordinary, this is just how it is, and it was like meeting an interesting stranger in the park. It set about to answer my question. It showed me two sections of neuronal connections. One was the overgrown environment of neurons spread like weeds from repeated exposure to the addictive behaviour. The other was the sparse orderly network of the control centres, the regulation features. It showed me the simplicity of behavioural addictions, be them chemical or conceptual. Once the addicting neuronal forests are more densely populated than the controlling behaviour regulating sections, then the system is out of balance and it requires more than a simple decision-to-stop to be free from the lure of the addiction. So simple. I understood and was grateful for the insight. As I went to leave, it basically asked, "well since you're here, and since you asked, would you like me to rewire your brain for you, and trim down this mess in your addiction centres so that you have a choice next time" ... This placed me straight into the books of Rick Strassman, who noticed that many of his DMT volunteers reported having their brains re-wired. I read this some years later. The experience is quite common. Interesting that, isn't it!

THE DANGERS OF NOT UNDERSTANDING THE POWERS OF MAGIC IN THE AGE OF REASON.

So, here we are, in the early phases of the exponential curve in technological advancement. Things are hotting up, racing ahead and about to get really interesting. We have the head of AI of Google, Ray Kurzweil telling us that by 2030 we'll be augmented with biomachine interfaces linking us to the cloud and all sorts of funky sci-fi stuff. So entrenched are we in the age of reason, so potent and overwhelming has it become, that perhaps we are racing a bit ahead of ourselves....

For example, there is something called "The Central Paradox" in quantum mechanics, and it's essentially about how single light photons or single electrons can make wave interference patterns, but when "observed" they collapse and return to particulate patterns instead. In over 100 years of examination of this problem, precisely zero philosophical progress in "understanding or interpreting" the results have been made. This clearly shows us that there are massive gaping holes in our scientific understanding of the universe at large. I do mean gaping holes, not some small details waiting to be tidied up. There is that cat in the box Schrodinger paradox too, and they go on. More recently at the edge of scientific enquiry we've discovered that either time can go backwards, or the order of time can be reversed, whatever the case these new discoveries violate an essential scientific cornerstone, that of causality. So a bit like "pop will eat itself" science is essentially beginning to destroy the very paradigm from which it was itself spawned, but only at the very edges of the known. It still works well enough to give us the internet and steam engines and rocket ships. However its eventual failure is guaranteed, or its limits will soon be reached and a new discipline will have to emerge. That discipline, I speculate will have to incorporate consciousness as part of its paradigm, and from where I am sitting that looks an awful lot like the discipline of magic. This may hold some degree of wisdom, science lacks wisdom, lacks empathy, and zero ability to provide any philosophical framework.

Where it perhaps becomes important, vitally important to incorporate aspects of magic with science is at the very cutting edge of science, because there they "may" matter. What do I mean by this?

To much fanfare in 2013 the team at the Large Hadron collider announced that they had "discovered" the famed Higgs Boson, and threw a big party. Today, a little BBC news article (see http://www.bbc.co.uk/news/science-environment-36976777) quietly states "New particle hopes fade as LHC data "bump" disappears". They thought they'd discovered a new particle, one they had been searching for, and it "appeared" coincidentally in their data with two separate detectors picking it up at the exact same time, making convincing scientific argument for the discovery. Later on those statistical anomalies vanished and there was nothing left but random noise and frustrated scientists.

You see, what *some* scientists know and *all* magicians know, but *most* scientists don't know, is that randomness can be easily influenced by consciousness. (See the Princeton Engineering Anomalies research labs). I doubt the CERN LHC scientists are the type of scientist to know this. So, here we have a bunch of 2,000 or so dedicated, cerebral, highly focussed, highly motivated LHC scientists, looking for a thing in a sea of randomness. They will have their careers made if they discover it, and want it so badly they go home and dream about finding it at night. What happens to the randomness of the collision data? Well, I speculate that, upon observation, it suddenly reveals bumps in the place they've been yearning to see bumps, and lo and behold they think they have found a new bit of fundamental physics, but instead they've been unwittingly influencing the statistics because they are totally unaware of their power to do so. Once "discovered" the focus on discovery, the dogged focus on the data is released, and "by magic" it all vanishes... leaving them bewildered and confused.

Have a look at the PEAR (see http://www.princeton.edu/~pear/) website if you can, it's really cutting edge, showing unequivocal empirical "proof" of a mind/matter influencing interface between quantum based random chaotic systems and consciousness.

THE INHERENCY OF THE UNOBSERVABLE NATURE OF THE MAGICAL RESULT

There is a certain black-box nature to magic as well, and it's something I doubt any of us will ever be able to solve satisfactorily. It's certainly a frustration I feel with magic as a system, but not too technical and easy enough to follow.

Say you do some magic to try make such and such happen. Say it happens. Can you ever attribute the desired and requested event to the magic performed, or was it simply that you saw it coming?

A great example of this problem comes from one of my beloved Sisters in the IOT. She did some magic to "find a fiver, at a particular location". So, not just find a fiver, but find a fiver here in this spot to prove the efficacy of her own magic ability. And, sure enough she did. So when we ask the question was it really the magic affecting her existential reality, or, was it that she could peek the future and see it coming, is an unanswerable quandary. You could keep putting it down to "coincidences" but that crutch wears thin after a bit. You know you're doing "something" to your reality, but what?

As pragmatist and scientist, I always try to keep things as simple as possible, delineate all phenomenon and then stick said phenomenon in isolation boxes with links between the isolated parts, and this works fine for technology and kind of works okay for biology, for a bit. What is it that magic is actually doing? I mean what function or aspect of reality is "my magical Will" having on the world, what bit of the world is it interfering with? Disincarnate spirit helpers working for me on the astral plane aside, I conclude that the aspect of reality that magic deals with directly is the Schrodinger probability wave function. Of this I am not able to say anything other than "May the odds be forever in your Favour". This short communication can't cope with a trip on the back of the twin coiled serpent of the probability wave function, the nature of information and the idea of state changes, but I promise to deliver, if such a request is made.

HOW DO WE "DO" MAGIC IN THE AGE OF REASON.

To finish, I'll give you an example of how I did my last magic ritual, and the purpose of it, and the overtly dramatic "props" that I used. The addition of theatre to my work is a very important aspect of it, if for nothing else I like dressing up in black hooded robes because it makes me feel cool-as-fuck.

So, my last magic …. Yesterday actually. A while ago, a Brother gave me a "totally legal" form of LSD called 1P-LSD, some kind of analogue whose subjective effects are indistinguishable from the original 25 form. Anyway, I give a few hits of this to my martial arts teacher, and his beautiful wife. They trot off into the wilderness and that is the last I think of it. Yesterday, they return and break my siesta, my beloved extended afternoon nap. Of course I am happy to see them, saucers for eye balls and big cheesy massive grins on their faces. They'd been playing in the park, on the swings and the slides, running thru the local woods, basking in the final days of the August full-summer sunshine. Magic can be spontaneous. I realised these two were tripping balls, and exuding excessive psychic energy, since I got a contact high from sitting with them. Time for magic, I thought... But what? I invited them to come with me to the top of the Winter Hill, a place they are both familiar with and love. They eagerly agreed. At that moment, the weather changed, for the worse, and began a storm. I drove to the hill, then beyond the "forbidden no vehicles beyond this point" sign and continued up the steep narrow winding country lane. Desolate moorland not clearly visible as the weather continued to deteriorate. Rain lashed on my windscreen, and visibility was poor, as we entered the cloud layer. There before me, in the clouds, looking like a dead ringer for the eye of Sauron, was the Transmitter Tower, the highest structure in the North West of England, its eerie red lights illuminating the swirling storm clouds around them in the black starless sky. I continued my approach with my passengers, still tripping and having fun, and totally unaware of my plan to utilise their state as a pre-amplification, for something "big...".

Upon arrival right next to the tower, opening the car doors, even the Border Collie so keen on the outdoors took one look at the weather, and opted to remain in the car... The tower looks like something as far removed from the natural world as can be. Metal on metal, oversized, bordering on menacing, certainly potent, vanishing completely in the cloud, only its lower substructures and supporting beams visible...

"Will you help me to save the world" I asked the girl a tad dramatically. She looked at me, her pupils madly dilated, "How?"... she asked....

So, I outlined to my tripping companions that I was keen to use their heightened lysergised state to help my magical will to make contact with the carrier wave signal from the Tower, modulate it and make instant contact with the 6.3 million people that it feeds a constant stream of information and misinformation to over a 40-mile radius. They agreed. I told them that my telepathic signal was simply "for them to be wonderful to each other". That was the statement of intent. The Winter Hill Tower, you must agree is quite the magic wand to use...

Weather now howling for added dramatic effect, rain in torrents... the red glow of the tower lights spooky as anything, threatening and ominous, Shouting over the storm....

"It is our will to utilise the carrier wave signal of this tower and subvert it for our own pirate transmission. To merge with the electromagnetic waves and to modulate them as a psychic communication, and thus influence the minds of 6.2 million people to behave and act wonderfully towards each other!"

Some chanting and arm waving later, a little so mote it be, and soaking wet, a quick banishing with "Pirates"... har har mee mayties.... and that was that...

This is magic in the age of reason.

The Zen of Chaos
Frater Pelagius

I was at the Thelemic symposium held in Oxford a couple of years ago, chatting away to one of the keynote speakers about the state of contemporary occultism. When the thorny (or perhaps horny) issue of Chaos Magick raised its head, he contrasted his own magickal current with a chaos magick that flitted from tradition to tradition leaving no time for the development of spiritual richness and depth.

Hey, I'm a nice guy. I didn't snap back. I simply suggested that while shifting between paradigms was a hallmark of much Chaos practice, there were also many others whose journeys had led them to a deep engagement with a specific tradition or pantheon.

My own journey with the Chaos impulse started a good ten years before becoming a member of the IOT. Through the writings of Peter Carroll and Phil Hine I saw a style of working and an engagement with contemporary culture that produced the 'Ah-ha!' moment. In the midst of paganisms cluttered by belief, and an old style Thelema preoccupied with the minutiae of days gone by, here was an approach that kicked out the jams and surged with right-brain artistry.

Over the last ten years, a large part of my magickal activity has been focused upon co-running a small hearth with my good friend and magickal colleague Siegrune. In the course of the hearth's life we have sought to communicate with others about the particular style and focus of our work. In 2005 (prior to my joining the IOT) we produced a short article for the Kith of Yggdrasil's journal Sun Wheel outlining our approach. My rationale for sharing this article in this collection is that I think it illustrates nicely the way in which the Chaos current can inform and creatively shape a magickian's engagement with a tradition, aware and respectful of its deep roots and yet still peeking under the dashboard to look at the wiring!

My thanks go to Siegrune for kindly allowing me to share this co-written article. Its views do not necessarily reflect the views of the Kith of Yggdrasil, an organization of which our hearth proudly continues to be a part.

ZEN ODINISM – OR WHAT WE DO AND WHY WE DO IT

'What do we do? And, why do we do it?'

Not unreasonable questions, you might think, but in my experience these are the questions that belief often experiences as uncomfortable. Most of us coming to the heathen path will have been exposed (if only in a nominal sense) to some other form of religion—probably Christianity. So how do we move from the position of feeling inspired by a mythology/literature/ideal which isn't part of the mainstream of our society, to the place where we can formally pay homage (if not worship) to those things which are given form by the new philosophy we have embraced, and what should that exercise entail?

Lying at the heart of the question of what our spiritual expression should look, feel or sound like is ultimately our view of what the divine is. Are the Gods and Goddesses distinct beings, or are they encultured personifications of principles experienced in the universe (or are they both) and what do we think these beings or principles want from us? Is our simple acknowledgement of these beings or ideals the manner in which their presence is made more manifest in the universe?

There is a Zen saying that in order to undertake the path of awakening one needs 'great faith, great doubt and great courage'. In pondering the conundrums facing the heathen or pagan seeking to live in the 21st century, I thought that this was quite an apt summary of what we are seeking to embody in the Hearth of Odin the Wanderer.

The small number of us who meet to celebrate the turning of the year are moved at a profound level by the weightiness of the Northern aesthetic—its emphasis on honour, its sparseness and sense of stoicism. The Gods, Goddesses and Wights that we honour and follow are clearly within the Northern Mythos—and for us, meeting on the land, this makes sense at a primal level. Now, all this sounds fairly normal for anyone who has been to a blot or a hearth before, but what a visitor might be struck by, is that— hey, we don't say a lot, we spend most of our time sitting down, and we also (gasp) spend some of our time laughing.

But how is this 'Zen'? And why 'Zen and Odinism'?

As to the 'how', we deem what we are doing as Zen-related. 'Zen' is the Japanese translation of

'Chan' which in turn is the Chinese translation of the Sanskrit 'Dhyana' i.e. meditation. Now, meditation can mean many things, but I think the ideas of mindfulness, awareness, wakefulness and quiet receptivity are at the heart of the experience I am pointing to. In practice this means that after acknowledging the elements and directions and welcoming the Gods, Goddesses and Wights, we spend most of our time listening both to the inner stirrings of ourselves and to the spirit of place.

As to why 'Zen and Odinism', at a simple level it's a syncretism we like! We are not an over-talkative bunch and we feel somewhat burnt-out by either deconstructionism or magical go-getting. At a philosophical level, however, I think there are deep connections between the concept of the way of the warrior (or 'Bushido', the code of conduct followed by the samurai), developed under the inspiration of Zen, and the spiritual warriorship that the heathen path seeks to encourage. The concept of Runa or 'mystery' also requires acknowledgement of the incompleteness of our spiritual vision, and of the limits that language places on us. This sits well with the type of Zen-mind attitude encouraged through working with apparently nonsensical koans. (Have you read the Rune poems recently?)

To some this may all sound like New Age woolliness, but all I offer in our defence is that we are not saying that anyone else has to do likewise, and that due to the historic gaps in our source material, many of us are inevitably splicing our heathenry with Hermeticism, Wicca and Christianity without being conscious of it or honest about it. If we have to splice—and I think that we must, because it is impossible to erase a thousand years of ancestral experience—then let's do it consciously and explicitly rather than claiming a feeble historic precedent. We are not living in the same world that our heathen forbears inhabited and we can't reconstruct it absolutely, so let's run with that and dwell in the Now, rather than trying to occupy what is gone.

To sum up, we are trying to find out what we think, via the paradigm of the Northern Gods and Goddesses. Within the framework of the Nine Noble Virtues and using the deities as exemplars, we are trying to find a means of connecting to our spiritual selves in a way which resonates for us—and that means accepting the things we have learnt from other traditions rather than trying to eradicate them (a fruitless task) from our well of memory.

For us, Odin and Frigga embody the search for wisdom and understanding. When in the Grimnismol Odin says; 'Over Midgard [the world], Hugin and Munin [Odin's ravens, "thought" and "memory"] both each day set forth to fly: for Hugin I fear, lest he come not home. But for Munin my care is more,' he is saying that memory is the most valuable of assets. This doesn't mean, can't mean, only certain memories—it refers to everything of value which has been learned by our ancestors and, crucially, by ourselves.

Odin wandered Midgard, watching and learning. We want to do the same and we see this as the meaning of our hearth. So we do what seems to us best to create the conditions that make this possible.

Hence our silence.

POSTSCRIPT

This short article was first written over five years ago, and our hearth continues to evolve. The core practice of mindful sitting remains, but we have also deepened our use of trance technology and the healing use of runic galdr (or 'incantation'). The hearth continues to be a laboratory within which such explorations can take place.

Reflecting on this work, I'm struck by the way it embodies a contemporary integration of Chaos principles and the way in which my experience within the hearth parallels my experience in the IOT. The shared themes that continue to make the strongest impact on me are these:

The importance of a collaborative environment in which people can bring together their individual discoveries in order to test them out in a safe, accepting space that can also give you feedback about things that don't work so well. This is true in our hearth and also within the magickal laboratory that is the IOT.

Magickal practice emerges from a place of depth and research. Sometimes an absurd or playful ritual serves as a Zen master, loosening our seriousness, but we also need work that builds soul. A failure to do so will result in a Chaos Magick that embodies the excesses of postmodern culture rather than critiquing it.

Magick needs to ensure the balance between activity and stillness, acceptance and change, variety and familiarity. The chaos star has a void at its centre and the cultivation of the disciplines outlined in 'Liber MMM' allows access to the stillness from which true Magick in its many colours can proceed.

REFERENCES

Henry Adams Bellows (translator), *The Poetic Edda: The Mythological Poems* (Mineola NY: Dover, 2004).

Peter Carroll, 'Liber MMM', in: *Liber Null & Psychonaut* (Boston MA: Weiser, 1987), pp. 13-23.

From Caterpillar to Butterfly... A Magickal Metamorphosis

Soror Inkberry

To say my life has changed over the past few years would be an understatement. Three years ago I was introduced to Chaos Magick and the IOT by someone very close to me and I haven't looked back since; it has been a crazy journey of self-discovery and metamorphosis and it is one that I wouldn't change. It has had its ups and downs, but what I have learned has made me the person that sits here today doing something I never thought I would be doing; I'm writing something that you are now about to read. It's crazy when I sit here and think about it, so I won't dwell too long or it might not get written, but let me tell you about how I came to be here doing just that...

As I mentioned at the start, I was introduced to the concept of Chaos Magick and the IOT three years ago. I've always been interested in the more esoteric strands of life, but fell out of touch with it for a while (oh alright, I confess, about twenty years but that is another story, and really rather dull) so when Frater Cadsmeek told me about this form of magick my ears pricked up. Here was someone telling me about something that seemed to fit in with the way I think. Yes, rules are there in life, but really, does life have to be that rigid? Does magick have to fit in with that way of thinking too? On this day do this; do this ritual in this way; perform this spell in this manner, etc. So we chatted some more and he gave me a list of books which he had read, and he showed me the website of the British Isles' section of the IOT. My intrigue went up even more. Who were these people? What did I need to do to join? Would they even let me in? After all my actual practice was little; a bit of tarot and a newly excited interest. Was I the sort of person they would welcome? "Oh what the heck", I thought and applied and then waited....and got accepted as a novice! This was it, this little caterpillar was about to go through the most amazing metamorphosis beyond her wildest imagination...

Along with the acceptance came some instructions; what was expected of me as a novice within the IOT. I had to keep a diary and follow the Liber MMM as laid out in Peter Carroll's "Liber Null & Psychonaut", as well as keep in touch with my mentor who was there to guide me. I felt a mixture of trepidation and excitement. Just what was I getting myself into? I had never in my life taken such a risk or thrown myself out of my comfort zone in such a way. Little did I know that I would be doing quite a bit more of that the further I carried on along this path.

So here I was. A novice of the IOT. I went out and got my diary and started to fill it in each day with my thoughts and practices. I won't pretend I found it easy, the motionless and no-thought mediation were hard at the start. Oh sure, it sounds easy, lie still for a minimum of thirty minutes each day and clear your thoughts, but it really wasn't for me. Lying still, yep,

I could do that, but clearing my thoughts? Are you kidding me? My mind was like a whirlwind; a crazy-ass storm of emotions, thoughts, memories and fears and I was expected to clear these all away? I was supposed to lie there and have no thoughts? Well, I tried... at first it felt impossible. Things kept popping into my consciousness; tasks I needed to do, what I was wanting to have for my tea, whether I was doing this whole thing right... but gradually this faded. I felt serene, and that's when I started to feel the different sensations. It was like my mind and body were soaring... I started to feel different. This had a knock-on effect in my daily life. I would look at the world differently, no longer taking things for granted. And I was changing too... my metamorphosis was beginning. Each day I tried to do some form of magickal practice; a tarot reading, a rune casting or some sigil work. And the crazy thing? I started seeing results. I never wished for the moon, just little things, and these things happened. A bit of confidence when facing a challenging situation, issues my friend was facing to be resolved; that sort of thing. My confidence in myself grew. I don't just mean in a "hey look at me! I can do magick" type of way, far from it. This was something I didn't share publicly... this was just my journey. But I started to believe in myself. Baby steps, yes, but it was there. And this leads me onto another important milestone within my journey...

I've never really been a confident person. It's something that I expect many people relate to; the feeling of not being good enough for whatever was being attempted. I would think "why would I be chosen to do that task, after all I'm not any good?".

But while working through my MMM and chatting with my mentor I started to feel different, and this new found confidence was cemented when I went to my first ever temple meeting. I met some amazing people who greeted me with a hug and smile. Listened to me, advised me. They never once judged me. Never once told me I wasn't worthy of this… and that meant so much to me. It made me feel like I belonged. They weren't pushy, they weren't demanding, they just let me be me. At that first temple meeting that I attended I had prepared a ritual for a friend who was going through chemotherapy, and I wanted to help them through it. I had no idea what would happen, but the feelings I got when I stood there in front of a group of people who had been doing this for years was something I will never forget. They listened to me and followed my lead, and gave it their all. They didn't laugh, or mock me, they didn't criticise or belittle me. They actually respected me. And for me that was something that I had never felt before. I remember leaving to go home feeling like I was flying. Like I was on top of the world. I had found a group of people who liked me, who wanted me to be a part of their group. I was waiting for the catch, but there wasn't one. They were just a group of like-minded people who wanted to do magick. I couldn't wait for the next time we would meet up…

The months went by and my Liber MMM was going well, I was doing my motionless/no thought every day and it was getting easier to clear my mind (I did have days when I would struggle; being ill isn't the best foundation for this, or facing something that was stressful hindered it a bit), and my magickal work was getting better and I was starting to get more results. I loved filling my diary in, it was a way of seeing my development from my nervous first steps to what I was starting to achieve. The guidelines state that you have to undertake the Liber MMM for a minimum of six months before being considered being made up from a novice to a neophyte, and I never in my wildest dreams thought I would be achieving that, so I just pootled along enjoying my journey, meeting more and more amazing people who I regard as my extended family. I was initiated in October 2014. I became a neophyte, and rather than being the end of my journey it just started a new one... I am now learning even more about myself, what I want to do in my life and still stepping out of my comfort zone on a daily basis. Being asked to write a piece for this book was just one example of that.

It's weird really, I've spoken about how much more confident I have become, how my life has changed, but I won't lie and say I still don't have days when I feel low or not worthy of things... but one thing that magick and my IOT family have taught me is how to face these demons head on, and that I have an amazing support network out there. I had a major wobble last year following one of the most intense instances of self-discovery during a ritual. It was like the most intense therapy sessions you could ever imagine, and I faced some of my deepest, darkest demons and memories which I had buried away. I wanted to leave the IOT. I suddenly felt that I was not worthy of this love, caring and friendship that I was feeling. I felt that I was just some sympathy case, that it was all a joke to them. But I couldn't have been more wrong. Instead of forcing me into staying or leaving they encouraged me to delve into myself even more, to make my decision based on my thoughts and evaluation of what I had experienced, to decide my own future, and make my own decision. So I did. To face all of the sadness, fears, self-loathing and bitterness that I had been unwittingly storing inside myself for a lifetime in one go was terrifying, and yet, once I sat on my own, away from everyone I started to realise that I was stronger than that. That this was what has shaped me, and rather than letting it control me, or run away from it I need to face up to it and make it work for me. I have to know that this is who I am, and that there are people out there who DO care, who DO want to listen to me and help. That accept me for who I am, not for what they want me to be... and once I had realised this I got back in touch and said that leaving was not an option. I need these people to help me develop and hone my skills in facing my inner demons and get stronger. And do you know what? I am. I'm not perfect (heck, nobody is), but I know who I am now, and I know that magick has helped me become strong enough to face any trials that my life will continue to throw at me. I am finally getting my wings; transforming into a butterfly. A slightly chaotic one, yes, but that caterpillar from three years ago hasn't been forgotten, but is acknowledged as being the reason why I'm here, sat in front of my laptop having written what you have just read. So thank you, and I hope that one day you will become a butterfly just as I have, and that your new found wings will take you on a fabulous journey like I am heading out on. I don't know what the future holds, but I know I now have the tools to face whatever it may bring head on, and that I am surrounded by the most amazing family I have ever known.

The EHNB Working
Frater Geur

Chaos Magic offers a practical approach and tends to attract people because of its ability to deliver specific, material results. However, the principles of Chaos Magic also lend themselves to workings with a more abstract intent for the purposes of self-illumination. At Samhain, 2009, Frater Kamael and I presented the following ritual, which I hope might serve as an example of this kind of working.

We had both become interested in the theme of reincarnation and the question of what is supposedly passed from one incarnation to the next. In the various traditions of Buddhism, the self is not recognised as possessing any substantive existence or essence, so although the idea of reincarnation is an accepted part of Buddhism, the notion of a 'soul' passing from one body to the next is most definitely not! The traditional view is that a person's karma (their actions whilst they were alive and the effects of those actions) is passed from one lifetime to the next, rather than any individual spark of identity.

To see if we could shed some light on this idea we borrowed a magical working from the system of Enochian angel magic. This is an extensive and complicated system for the invocation of angelic spirits, derived from written records produced by the famous 16th-century mages Dr. John Dee and Edward Kelley. We decided to evoke the most powerful spirit within this system, known as EHNB (or 'Ey-Hey-Ney-

Bey') and ask it questions about our former incarnations. In particular, we were interested in finding out how each of us met our deaths in a previous existence, to see if this could shed any light on the karmic baggage we are dragging between lifetimes.

So now we had an intent and a system we'd elected to use, but the problem with Enochian magic is that it seems—at first glance—to depend upon a lot of intricate equipment and faffing around. It's also definitely not a spectator sport, and could prove boring to participants not directly involved in channelling and questioning the spirit. So we stripped the paraphernalia right back, and also devised a means to involve everyone in evoking and receiving illumination from EHNB.

Two sources proved particularly useful: DuQuette and Hyatt's *Enochian World of Aleister Crowley* (1991), which is an indispensable manual on Enochian magic (Golden Dawn style), including everything needed to ditch the faff and just get on with it; and also DuQuette's *My Life with the Spirits* (1999), a magical autobiography with many interesting anecdotes concerning Enochian magick, plus a chapter dedicated to EHNB and this spirit's supposed ability to reveal past lives.

Fortunately for us, another of the attractive qualities of EHNB is that aside from being the mightiest, it is also the easiest of the Enochian angels to evoke. The ritual involves the reading of two short invocations (known as 'The First and Second

Enochian Keys') and an even shorter conjuration to summon it to visible appearance. Kapow! Job done.

One component of the ritual that is indispensable, however, and cannot be rushed or economised is what happens between the spirit and the scryer—the person who conveys the spirit's message to the participants. The best approach, in my experience, is to adopt a loosely focused state of mind which, despite being relaxed, is nevertheless attentive to everything passing through. The only means of manifestation a spiritual being has is what we provide, so whatever arises to the mind in the presence of the spirit is the spirit. It is important not to get side-tracked into analysing intellectually what appears, or wondering if what it 'seems' is really what it 'is'. Get phenomenological on your own arse! Spirit is as spirit seems.

Personally speaking, when I open myself to a message from a non-embodied entity, usually what I receive is only a sense of some kind of intention, like a mental push in a vague direction but without any specific content. I receive a general sense of what the spirit intends, but must arrive at the specifics by encouraging the intention to clothe itself in visible signs. For me, emotional tone is the means of achieving this. An angry intention provokes different images in the mind from a sorrowful one, and inclines the mind toward different images and words. These usually suggest themselves automatically if I take my awareness meditatively into the intention, but they are not the original form in which the communication is expressed. I arrive at signs, but the original communication is an intention, and so often the signs arrived at are usually indirect or 'symbolic' rather than a direct form of speech.

I'm sure there are people far better at this than I am, but that's the way I do it and it obtains reasonable results. I recommend that anyone interested should practise this art as often as they can, test what they obtain, and in this way arrive at their own method for achieving usable results.

What follows is a transcript of the session, taken from an audio recording made at the time.

Photocopies from DuQuette & Hyatt of the four Enochian tables are positioned with candles in each of the quarters with a copy of the Tablet of Union in the centre. A short banishing ritual is performed and the statement of intent is declared: 'It is our will to evoke the Enochian angel EHNB to answer our questions in good faith.' Everyone takes part in chanting the name of the spirit, 'Ey-Hey-Ney-Bey', whilst at the same time Frater Kamael reads the First and Second Enochian Keys. Frater Geur sits in meditation posture with a thick cloth draped over his head and enters trance. Then the participants fall silent and Frater Kamael leads everyone in reciting the Enochian Conjuration, in a call and response fashion.

A long silence follows.

FRA KAMAEL: Fra Geur, are you getting anything?
Another long silence.

FRA GEUR: Can we have the conjuration again? I'm sorry...

Fra Kamael reads the conjuration again.

FRA GEUR: The spirit has taken on the form of Baphomet.

FRA KAMAEL: Thank you for being with us, EHNB. We have called you here so that you may answer our questions in good faith. Are you prepared to do so?

FRA GEUR: It's ready, but it's a lot more dour and serious than I was expecting. It's quite solemn. But, yeah, it's ready.

FRA KAMAEL: EHNB, is it okay to ask you questions about our past lives and how we might have died?

FRA GEUR: It's ready, but it is telling us not to take this lightly.

FRA KAMAEL: Oooooh! Why shouldn't we take it lightly?

FRA GEUR: It gave me a picture then of keys, and it seemed to be saying that this can go quite deep and unlock a lot of stuff.

FRA KAMAEL: Shall I go first?

FRA GEUR: Yep.

FRA KAMAEL: EHNB, who was I in my past life?

FRA GEUR: You were trying to go up too high. It's giving me weird images. It's like you were a winged man brought to earth.

FRA KAMAEL: Sounds like me. Can you get a name?

FRA GEUR: I can see epaulettes on a uniform, like a pilot's uniform. It's telling me that this person met their end by trying to do too much. There was someone in command, someone who should have taken a back seat, but they took a front seat and that's how you died.

FRA KAMAEL: Fair enough. Shall we move onto the next person?

Next person steps forward with Fra Kamael.

FRA GEUR: Right, the next person. I'm getting a really different vibe, which is of someone who was ill for a long time and had very few people left at the end of their life. This is someone who was sick and all the people around gradually dwindled away. There's quite a sense of despair and loss. As this person became more ill, the people were less able to be around them and the sense of loneliness and withdrawal grew worse.

FRA KAMAEL: The next person?

Next person steps forward.

FRA GEUR: This was someone doing something completely reckless to do with firearms! It looks to me as if they might have been playing Russian roulette, playing with their chances, and died in the midst of life in a way that was entirely their own fault—but they wouldn't have had it any other way.

Next person.

FRA KAMAEL: EHNB, what about this next person?

FRA GEUR: Oh! That was frightening! A sudden disease that afflicted the face... I think it might be plague or smallpox, but someone was struck down shockingly quickly and didn't have time to come to terms with what was happening to them. Definitely something around the face area... The idea that this person was deeply affected by the fact that they became unrecognisable to themselves at the end.

Next person.

This person was a mother, someone very maternal in their past life and loving and when they passed away their thoughts were focused on the people left behind rather than themselves. A sense that there wasn't any worry for themselves at all. The stress of dying was all concerned with thoughts of people they'd left behind.

Next person.

This next person must have been blind when they passed away. That's all I'm getting. Blind or very severely disabled. Sorry, it's not very clear.

Next person.

This person is interesting because they have a god or goddess who is very much on their side. It looks like some sort of Hindu deity. This is someone who has a very close affiliation with a certain god and took a lot of strength from that in the lifetime that I'm seeing and managed to find a lot of peace with their death because of this. I'm not sure what kind of deity it is but it looks tantric, Hindu or something like that. There is the idea that if they haven't already then this person should reconnect with that deity, because that seems to indicate something about their nature.

Next person.

There is a connection with the sea. A sense that this person has had the connection with the sea through more than one lifetime. This is someone who travelled the world a lot. There is a picture of a person in a white uniform, like a sailor, but the main sense is that this soul who continues to be reborn is a wanderer, a traveller, and this continues in each lifetime. A very restless person.

Next person.

I'm not getting much for this person. I'm not sure what I'm being shown. But... ah! There is a sense of anxiety, but this anxiety is created in the mind and wasn't part of reality. This was someone who worried a lot in their past life and made themselves ill. It's as if this person lived in a kind of 'bad reality' that they made for themselves and made things seem far worse than they actually were.

Next person.

[*Laughs.*] A strong connection with animals here. [*Laughs.*] As if this person was someone who lived with animals very closely—wild animals. Being close to wild animals expressed a big part of their personality for them. Images of wolves—those sort of animals. It's their personality rather than how they met their end that I'm seeing. This is someone who lived very near the edge of civilization and found it very fulfilling.

Next person.

I see a father in a hospital bed surrounded by children and grandchildren and very proud of his family; a real 'head of the family' figure. This was someone very fulfilled by that role and to and loved by all the people around him. It doesn't feel long since this incarnation ended.

Next person.

This person is interesting because they were involved with the creation of buildings, the rebuilding of a city, a city that has been destroyed, and this person has been involved in putting it back together on a monumental scale. I can't really get a sense of when this was; probably quite a long time ago. Perhaps ancient. But buildings and the environment and putting civilization together is what concerned this person. Their death is connected with what they did, but I think perhaps I'm reading too much into it at this point.

Next person.

I'm getting water imagery again and I think this person must've drowned but in very peaceful water on a summer's day, as if they were on holiday near a lake or something like that, and it was a really stupid accident that shouldn't have happened, at a really happy time in their life. They were taken away from this, but the happiness they had was taken over with them somehow. So although it was tragic, they could carry this happiness into future incarnations. This is a person with an underlying sense of calm who associated death with calmness. A paradox.

Next person.

This person died on an operating table in a hospital and there's a sensation that the surgeons who should have taken care of this person didn't care enough or do their jobs properly. They couldn't be bothered. Whether this person was extremely ill and wasn't expected to survive, or whether they were old— there's a real sense of this person passing away because others didn't do their best. This has carried into subsequent incarnations. It's not quite a fear, but a lingering expectation that people will let them down.

Next person.

The spirit is showing me imagery from the time of King Charles I, from before the Civil War. This person was an affluent aristocrat into fine living, but this is not an uncultured, hedonistic person. This was someone refined, contemporary and with real taste, but definitely someone who lived a very fine life and was interested in material enjoyments. I don't know how they died. It was just before the civil war, so maybe they died in that war on the Royalist side.

Next person.

This person died with a lot of other people in traumatic circumstances.

FRA KAMAEL: It wasn't on a ship, was it?

FRA GEUR: I don't think so. It's difficult to say if it was an accident or war, but a real sense of panic and fear.

FRA KAMAEL: Is there anything you can tell us about this person's life?

FRA GEUR: The main thing I'm being shown is that a lot of people died at the same time. It doesn't seem that old. It seems twentieth century imagery. There might have been some sort of musical connection. I'm being shown a musical instrument, but there's not a lot of detail there.

Next person.

A young woman. She didn't have any children when she died and experienced that as a loss, and this was carried over into subsequent lives, about not having any children and the need to do something about that in the lives that followed.

FRA KAMAEL: You've mentioned a few times about future lives. Does that mean you have knowledge of future incarnations?

FRA GEUR: I get the feeling that the spirit is showing important incarnations that weren't necessarily the last one.

FRA KAMAEL: Okay. I have one final question, EHNB. Who was Fra Geur in his past life and how did he die?

FRA GEUR: There's an image of a deserted house and he is left alone in this house, but he's not old when he dies. It's as if this house is falling down all around him and all the money has gone and he can't control what's happening any more. He is just going into a decline.

FRA KAMAEL: Okay EHNB, thank you very much for attending this evening. We've found the information very helpful. Depart this place now in peace. Thank you very much for coming. Are you alright, Fra Geur?

FRA GEUR: Yes. He's gone.

A final banishing ritual is performed and the ritual is closed.

It's important to appreciate how it's best not to treat the results of a working like this as 'facts'. Rituals for self-illumination are a means of producing information for consideration rather than material we're obliged to accept as a literal truth, which would be a sure-fire recipe for paranoia and psychosis. Information obtained should always be tested, 'tried on', and retained only if it proves valid or useful, otherwise it does no harm to throw it away, forget about it, or file it away in a drawer somewhere until the day arrives (or not) when suddenly it makes more sense.

After the ritual I was surprised by the number of participants who approached me to comment on the relevance of EHNB's communication. The person who 'worked with wild animals' in a previous life had (unbeknownst to everyone present) worked with them also in his current life; the person who had 'died blind and disabled' had been told the very same thing previously by psychics; and the person who had 'enjoyed a connection with a tantric deity' stated that this was indeed something that resonated with him. And there were other interesting connections besides.

What this illuminated was how the doctrine of reincarnation has value only if it elucidates issues in our current lives. Few of us (if any) have conscious memories of having lived before, so we can identify a past life as being 'ours' only to the extent that it reflects or reacts with issues in the life we're living now. This is what the notion of our karma being reborn (not our 'souls') is all about; it's the issues and effects of the life we live now that survive the extinction of individual consciousness and are transferred onwards. Consciousness in itself has no impact on the world; our issues and effects are our legacy—what else could there be? To the extent that we recognise these in the story of an individual life we might say that life was 'ours'.

Just as interesting were the people who found no connection whatsoever with EHNB's communication. We might say that this is because the 'communication' was merely a fantasy on the scryer's part; or—more deviously—that the issues EHNB described were being unconsciously denied by the person concerned. But in any case, what's clear is that there has to be some kind of resonance between EHNB's message and the issues (karma) that the person is confronting now, otherwise there's no sense of connection at all.

Whether this connection does indeed constitute some kind of tangible link with the consciousness of a historical individual is a difficult problem to tackle. Aleister Crowley had no qualms about it; he boldly declared himself the reincarnation of Edward Kelley, the man who fulfilled the role of Dr. John Dee's scryer during the original Enochian workings. Yet Frater Kamael has pointed out to me that perhaps Crowley doesn't have a monopoly on such claims.

EHNB told Frater Kamael: 'you were going up too high... it's like you were a winged man brought down to earth.' At the time, he took this as an allusion to his habitual tendency to overachieve, but it's also a curious echo of how Edward Kelley met his death: it's said that Kelley fell from a tower in his attempt to escape from Hněvín Castle in the Czech Republic, where he had been imprisoned after convincing local nobles he could create gold.

Dee's death was less dramatic. He spent his final years at home in poverty, gradually forced to sell his possessions in order to support himself and his sole remaining daughter. EHNB's description of my death resonated with a stubborn habit I have of isolating myself, but there's a tempting historical parallel that could also be drawn here: 'It's as if this house is falling down all around him and all the money has gone and he can't control what's happening any more. He is just going into a decline.'

REFERENCES

Lon Milo DuQuette & Christopher S. Hyatt, *Enochian World of Aleister Crowley* (Tempe, AZ: New Falcon, 1991) .

Lon Milo DuQuette, *My Life with the Spirits* (York Beach, ME: Red Wheel / Weiser, 1999).

Baphomet Rising
Sator Julian

In the centre of the circle one of the black figures is raving, shouting guttural unearthly gibberish. Pacing the perimeter of the space others cry out. The atmosphere is greasy with the static-like shimmering of magickal power. A force is welling up, stooping down, invading and opening each cell of the wizard at the centre of the temple.

There is a howl like a beast, a laugh, a yawn and the company fall silent. Baphomet is here!

So who is this deity of the sorcerers, Baphomet?

The notoriety of the name begins with The Knights Templar, specifically through confessions provided during their persecution in the early 1300s. Only a small number of The Poor Knights ever confessed to anything that smelt clearly heretical, an even smaller number named the focus of their idolatry as Baphomet. The word itself, though arguably little more than a European corruption of the name Mohammed, possesses a remarkable quality. Around these eight letters have gathered a concretion of esoteric meaning and conspiratorial uncertainty. 'Father of the temple of peace of all men' is one rendition, 'Baptism of Wisdom' is another, 'mother of breath' a third. It is as though, through a game of Chinese whispers, these few syllables have mutated into the key to a far-reaching secret knowledge.

For the besmirched Templars, hungry and tortured with fire, this Baphomet had appeared in a variety of forms: a cat, a many-faced figure, a skull stuffed with grain. In no account do we find anything at all similar to the innumerable horned devils that populate a modern Google search for images of the name Baphomet.

Historians have long contested the origins and meaning of the Templar trials. Was it all a put-up job by Philip the Fair of France (aided and abetted by the excommunicated, heresy-obsessed Guilliaume de Norgaret)? Or was there really some dark secret? No smoke without Hell-fire and all that... Suggestions that the Templars were secretly in league with the Muslims, that they had absorbed the mythology of the Middle East into their own sodomitic initiations, abounded. However even something as stable as history has a habit of rewriting itself. In 2007 documents were discovered in the Vatican archive that demonstrated how the weakling Pope Clement of the time really didn't think the Order was guilty at all. So one can never be quite certain of the facts in a case like this. Especially since the very nature of secret organisations (and the Templars certainly maintained esoteric initiatory practices if nothing else) is of clouded realities and oblique disclosures. Like the Old Man of the Mountains would say, 'Nothing is True, Everything is Permitted'.

After the trials, the sequestration of assets and the public immolations outside Notre Dame, the Templars were finished. Or at least that's what the sober, non-conspiracy theorist historians tend to suggest. Vague mentions are made of the fact that some Templar groups might have dispersed to areas outside of Papal control. Scotland is a favoured spot, though again historians are at pains to point out that structures such as the enigmatic Rosslyn Chapel are much later (around 1446). It may well be inspired by Templar iconography but is not directly linked. The same is true, one might argue, for the earlier mysterious ritual chamber, Royston Cave.

This conical cave, carved from the chalk beneath the crossroads of two Roman roads, certainly evidences Templar imagery. St. Catherine (the Christian take on Hypatia), armed knights and crosses are hewn into the lower section of the chamber. Then there is the Freemasonic iconography on the walls. Suns and moons are carved above 'the grave', a depression in the earth against one edge of the octagonal floor. This lies beneath the level of what was once a six-pointed star-shaped wooden floor. The original visitors to the chamber would have alighted on the star first, before making their descent to the lower regions. A large cresset provided illumination for the ceremonies that would have been held there. Above ground, the smoke vented through the chimney of a building that occasionally served as a hunting lodge. Of course what exactly went on in the lodge or the chamber remains a mystery, and a literal lineage with the Templars might be impossible to prove. But such proof is unnecessary and misses the point. To give a modern example: museums around the world often find they own bones from tribal cultures that were collected (to use the polite term) from far distant lands. In these cases the British governing body for museums suggests that the 'actual descendants' have a claim on these objects and it is proper for the museum to enter into negotiations should that culture want the remains of their ancestors returned. Not only 'actual' but also 'cultural descendants' have such a claim. In other words, a modern Pagan would have a basis to argue for the return of ancient Pagan material from a public collection (especially in the case of human remains, where the intention would be lay them to rest in a manner sanctioned by that religion). So Royston Caves and Rosslyn Chapel may not be 'actual' but are undoubtedly 'cultural' descendants of the Knights.

Of course magicians, being a band of scandalous rouges, liars and geniuses, have always been happy to claim cultural ancestry with anyone who looks a little outré. Baphomet is one name that makes its descent through this Bohemian lineage. Moreover as a Google image search will show, as time moves, so this Deity of the Sorcerers finds earlier and earlier roots. No longer trapped in the medieval, Baphomet seems to retroactively appear as the dancing sorcerer in cave art, or the antlered figure on the Gundestrup cauldron.

Why is Baphomet so horny? Goat horns are the most popular by a long way, but as this entity shades of into the God of the Witch Cult (of Murrayite, Wiccan or teen varieties), stag's horns rise up instead. The genesis of the horned god, like most of magick, comes together all on its own. Elements are drawn from the wild writings of Joseph von Hammer-Purgstall who allegedly discovered some 'Baphomets' in the Imperial Museum of Vienna. One of them sports a ram's horns; the other with upraised arms, holds the sun and moon and at its foot is a pentagram and seven-rayed star. Later the horns became essential in the fabulous fraud of Léo Taxil, who created a monstrous Masonic conspiracy that he fed to the credulous French public (and even more credulous Catholic clergy). Taxil alleged that unspeakable debauchery took place in Masonic lodges. These orgies were presided over by a devilish and (naturally) horned Baphomet. In addition to moral dereliction, Taxil claimed that the Masons were part of a revolutionary plot to destroy France and lay the foundations for a one-world government. He kept the gag up for nearly twelve years, when (as his stories became progressively weirder, but not before the Pope had congratulated him on his work) he revealed, to a packed press conference that he'd made it all up. The audience didn't take kindly to the punch line, and Taxil had to be escorted from the venue with a police guard.

Then we have Eliphas Levi, granddaddy of modern occultism. Levi spills plenty of ink on Baphomet. Here's what he had to say in Transcendental Magic:

"The goat which is represented in our frontispiece bears upon its forehead the Sign of the Pentagram with one point in the ascendant, which is sufficient to distinguish it as a symbol of the light. Moreover, the sign of occultism is made with both hands, pointing upward to the white moon of CHESED, and downward to the black moon of

GEBURAH. This sign expresses the perfect concord between mercy and justice. One of the arms is feminine and the other masculine, as in the androgyne of Khunrath, whose attributes we have combined with those of our goat, since they are one and the same symbol. The torch of intelligence burning between the horns is the magical light of universal equilibrium; it is also the type of the soul exalted above matter, even while cleaving to matter, as the flame cleaves to the torch. The monstrous head of the animal expresses horror of sin, for which the material agent, alone responsible, must alone and for ever bear the penalty, because the soul is impassable in its nature and can suffer only by materializing. The caduceus, which replaces the generative organ, represents eternal life; the scale-covered belly typifies water; the circle above it is the atmosphere, the feathers still higher up signify the volatile; lastly, humanity is depicted by the two breasts and the androgyny arms of this sphinx of the occult sciences." – (Levi 2001 : 308-9)

Baphomet is for Levi the central 'object of adoration in the secret rites' (Levi 2001:14). For him this image is at the core of occultism. His now famous image of the Goat of Mendes represents the alchemical union of opposites. Solve and Coagula neatly tattooed on those arms—dissolve and recombine, something Baphomet clearly has a genius for. But what, one wonders, are these 'secret rites'?

Of course some people just can't let go of all that conspiratorial tosh that Taxil wrote (even after he revealed his joke many suspected he'd been bought off by the Masonic conspiracy). And this attitude persists, indeed has grown, in the modern age. Fed by the lightning-quick rumour mill of the internet, what are perhaps only superficial similarities between objects become firm connections. Is this the reality of being a 'cultural descendant' mentioned earlier, or simply the growing madness of incipient schizophrenia?

Do the figures here look at all similar to you? One is the first president of the United States of America, the other is George Washington.

Back to our magicians, screaming in the temple. Why are they invoking this spirit? What's the deal with this Devil?

Crowley's recension of the magical tradition in his cult of Thelema namechecks our horned deity. 'The Gnostic Mass', given by Crowley in Liber XV, names Baphomet: 'And I believe in the Serpent and the Lion, Mystery of Mystery, in His name BAPHOMET' (Kaczynski 2009: 50). However, even though Baphomet gets a big shout (in a volume that bears one of its numbers—XV is the number of 'The Devil' tarot card) our mysterious god isn't really centre-stage.

Although apparently ripe for the picking, Baphomet only appears as a minor player in Thelema, and in the emerging witchcraft movement other horned Lords were preferred. We had to wait until Baphomet inspired Pete Carroll during the early days of the Magical Pact of the Illuminates of Thanateros (the name itself, 'The Pact', cries out for a devil to be present at proceedings). Other deities were in the frame: Hermes Trismegistus and Abaraxas. But it was Baphomet who got the job (or obsessed Carroll's mind most successfully). Carroll writes:

"Baphomet is the psychic field generated by the totality of living beings on this planet. Since the Shamanic aeon, it has been variously represented as Pan, Pangenitor, Pamphage, All-Begetter, All-Destroyer, as Shiva-Kali—creative phallus and abominable mother and destroyer—as Abraxas—polymorphic god who is both good and evil—as the animal headed Devil of sex and death, as the evil Archon set over this world, as Ishtar or Astaroth—goddess of love and war— as the Anima Mundi or World soul, or simply as 'Goddess.' Other representations include the Eagle, or Baron Samedi, or Thanateros, or Cernunnos—the horned god of the Celts." – (Carroll 1987: 158)

So Baphomet, according to this formulation, is the androgynous fusion of above and below. Devil and God in one image. Moreover Carroll points to the roots of this deity as many chaos magicians understand it: as the totality of living entities; Baphomet is the biosphere, the life-force on earth. The union of opposites that it represents is the union of the DNA helix, the twisted double serpent that hides in the core of our cells. It is the eater and the eaten, and a reminder that, in turn, that which devours shall also be devoured.

Within the IOT Baphomet is the personification of chaos. The mysterious space, the Kia, out of which flood the ten thousand things. Baphomet also represents the emerging paradigms of magic. The core ritual that calls upon this spirit, 'The Mass of Chaos B', details the five forms through which it appears in successive aeons. In the shamanic aeon it is the undifferentiated Great Spirit. Then as agriculture emerges it is transformed into the horned god of fertility. Then, cast down by patriarchy, Baphomet is twisted into devilish form, and as reductionist science develops, it disappears in a puff of logic. Then, in our age, the hidden god bursts back onto the stage, yelling and dancing and exhorting us to understand that all things are alive. A panpsychic prophet whose messages are appearing in physics, in biology, in art and in magick.

It is 10:30am, in central London. A man dressed as Baphomet is drumming wildly in Trafalgar square. On the edge of a high plinth he leans out and throws seeds and petals onto the concrete below. Sycamores cut whirling crescents through the air, daisy petals float in the bright sun-shine. The black form, horns rising bold against the white stone of the National Portrait Gallery, reaches down. It picks up a rose and casts it towards the earth. Again and again it casts the thorned, red crowned stems into the air. Quizzical tourists look on as their open-top bus drives past. A woman is overheard to say to her child, 'Look what Baphomet is doing up there darling!' A magician mutters, 'Jacques du Molay, thou art avenged!'

And that Illuminati conspiracy? What of that? Eliphas Levi asks:

"What then is taking place in the world, and why do priests and potentates tremble? What secret power threatens tiaras and crowns?" – (Levi 2001 : 8)

Baphomet is the deity of the now and of the future. Pregnant with power and mythologically mutable, unifying truth and falsehood. Baphomet is precisely located at the root of modernity's love of conspiracy. And what is that conspiracy that makes the crowned head lie uneasy? Perhaps it is that greatest of rebellions articulated by Socrates and Leary: 'Think for yourself, question authority'. Because we are all Baphomet, and there is no part of us that is not of the gods. The divine exists, and as the rushing force of chaos, it is right here, right now.

REFERENCES

Peter J. Carroll, *Liber Null & Psychonaut* (York Beach, ME: Red Wheel / Weiser, 1987).

Richard Kaczynski, *The Weiser Concise Guide to Aleister Crowley* (San Francisco, CA: Red Wheel/Weiser, 2009).

Eliphas Levi, *Transcendental Magic*, translated by A.E. Waite (York Beach, ME: Weiser, 2001).

Nikki Wyrd & Julian Vayne, *The Book of Baphomet* (Mandrake of Oxford, 2012).

The Magical Pact of the Illuminates of Thanateros

The Kite

When does anyone ever say 'The Magical Pact of the Illuminates of Thanateros'? I mean, what is a mouthful like that for? Why 'Pact', rather than 'Order'? What's a 'Thanateros' anyway? And why 'Illuminates,' when they mostly seem to prefer rock 'n' roll sorcery to climbing the mystic ladder? Let's unpack this title and get some goodies out of it.

Before we do, let's reckon on some disagreement. Your working chaos magician thrives on diversity and you can't rely on him or her to agree with what they said last month, never mind with what anyone else says. As the journal Chaos International puts it, the views published 'are not necessarily in accord with the beliefs of the Editor at the time of publication'. Pete Carroll, one of the founders of this approach to magic, may himself fail to recognise clearly his co-creation in the description that follows, but hopefully he'll see in it the fulfilment of his wish that we don't slavishly follow his genius but employ our own in order to surpass our past.

And then, of course, some would call what follows an ideal rather than a description of the Pact. Whatever their criticism, I call on them to consider this treatment a reminder, even a challenge. In the end, though, I wouldn't want you to treat this as an argument for any particular interpretation. I long ago gave up on debate as a vainglorious exercise in winning points rather than hearts. I'd rather we walked together in a rich garden of ideas, enjoying the view and breathing the fresh air of Chaos. My garden is actually a labyrinth, but if we unravel my title as a thread we won't get lost. Let's stroll, shall we?

The Illuminates of Thanateros (IOT) describes itself as a Pact. Let's define a 'pact' as 'the agreement of a collection of free individuals to act together in each other's interest'. Those individuals could range from business associates to heads of state, coming together for commercial, political and military, or—as in this case—magical purposes. In the West we have a stereotype of solitary sorcerers summoning up unfriendly demons and binding them with a pact. Yes, tongue-in-cheek this sound like a fair description of chaos magicians: the cats you cannot herd, individualists, challenging the boundaries, and occasionally demonic in aspect. Oh the stories we could tell!

'Acting together in each other's' interests.' In eons past shamans, witches and witch doctors, medicine men and women—whatever they called themselves—held a place in their semi-nomadic societies. They had the tribally sanctioned job of communicating with the Otherworld and retrieving resources of healing, hunting, blessing and cursing for the tribe. Modern anthropology has described a number of such societies from which we deduce what we can of our prehistoric forebears.

However, modern society has no place for us and does not support our endeavour. We have no tribe for whom to work our magic, and without such a context we doom ourselves to what our society generally regards as irrelevant, stupid superstition. Even individualists like us need at the very least a peer group with whom to share our discoveries and from whom to receive the reality check which may preserve our sanity, for our society thinks we're nuts and will pressure us, subtly or brutally, to backslide into mundane conformity or else to nosedive into mental breakdown. A given magician might survive alone, but perhaps at great personal cost and at the expense of the fullness of magical development.

So, lacking a supportive culture, we create a supportive subculture. I don't mean you to think of the Pact as some sort of support group, but support I definitely find, in the form of the reality check, and a shared context for my explorations and a spur to progress. And of course, we participate in each other's magic, always a learning experience which makes possible more variety of magics than we might attempt alone. And some wicked, intense times.

Pete Carroll and company chose to call the IOT a pact rather than an order, yet it has some of the structures of a magical order, here defined as an organization for facilitating group magic. Some people, myself included, find off-putting robes, fancy names, initiation rites, passwords and secrets. But while I don't really care for the Masonic vestiges as such, I notice that these theatrical touches of robes and ceremony—props and cozzies—do seem to ease the diverse group into solidarity for the business of the hour.

Then again, the Pact resembles a family, which I define as a bunch of people most of whom you didn't choose to belong among, some of whom you can't stand, many of whom you have to work to get on with. Again, we use terms borrowed from initiatory cults, such as 'Frater' and 'Soror'—'brother' and 'sister' to you and me. Given the history of ego-driven infighting amongst occultists of all stripes, a consciousness of our solidarity seems necessary both for our collective well-being and our effectiveness when in action. Call me 'Frater,' and mean it. After all, when I hear some new Initiate 'offer to the Pact such powers of will, imagination, perception and concentration as I possess', I take it personally and remember how I offered this and every Initiate the same when I first spoke those words years before.

At this point, I'd like us to pause and savour the scents of this part of the garden with a magical incantation. Now that you know what I mean by 'the Pact'—a family, a supportive subculture, a collection of free individuals who agree to act together in each other's interest in an organization for facilitating group magic—let's consider the Ouranian Barbaric expression: GOBCHURINOR FOUIJA. It's usually translated 'Big Love,' but we've now unpacked a pretty full meaning from it. So take a deep breath as you bring to mind the nature of the Pact, and say deliberately 'GOBCHURINOR FOUIJA.' Go on. It won't take a moment. Savour it.

A word here about grades, another Masonic vestige. In many another organization grades appear as evidence of rank, and in our game specifically as marks of 'progress'. Clearly these notions have no place in a Pact, 'a collection of free individuals' as you recall. In the IOT, grades function as markers of depth of involvement in the organization. As Novices we work to join this august company, focussing on our personal magical development and finding out if our face fits, culminating in our recognition by the Pact as Neophytes. As Neophytes, we may wish to broaden our Novitiate focus with group work and a fuller contribution, culminating in our recognition as permanent Initiates. Most happily remain here, but the grade of Adept takes us into a whole new level, recognising us as experienced and skilful magicians and presenting us with the duty of using these skills to inspire others and give leadership, but challenging us also with the burden of administration. Finally, the Pact bestows the degree of Magus upon one whose commitment to the Pact works at an international level.

So we have a Magical Pact, a collection of free individuals who agree to act together in each other's interest in an organization for facilitating group magic. 'I thought you guys were chaos magicians?' I might hear you ask. 'Isn't "chaos organization" a contradiction in terms?'

Our approach to magic was nearly called 'results magic' on account of its usual focus. This comprises part of the reality check of which I have spoken. After all, if you're making excuses for not getting results then you're fooling yourself about your magical prowess, yes? However, at some point a vogue for chaos mathematics—the science of aiding the linear processes of human thinking to describe the innumerable non-linear processes of the universe— seemed to offer a useful metaphor for magic, as well as suggesting a hip scientific glamour. Mythological 'Chaos' refers not to disorder where one might expect order, but to the primeval unformed potential that awaits realisation—making real, as in creation from Chaos, all things from 'no-thing.'

In our contemplation of magic, we discern a continual in-out movement, an arising from oblivion into manifestation, and a falling from manifestation into oblivion, creation and destruction, birth and death, arising and passing away, at all levels from the most fleeting impression to perhaps the life-cycle of the universe itself, a fractal—self-similar at all scales—process of coming together and falling apart, solve et coagula, non-linear—multiple beginnings and multiple endings beyond our capacity to apprehend all at once. As above, so below, indeed.

This movement, this vast and complex interwoven cluster of processes we describe by the ancient Greek mythological titles of Eros and Thanatos. Eros, the principle of springing into abounding life. Thanatos, the principle of inevitably decaying. Unfortunately, many magicians seem to have read Pete Carroll's comments about Sex and Death as characteristic magical trances and have not performed his Thanateros Rite, which puts those trances into clearer and greater perspective. I recommend you research it. As magicians we seek to participate actively in the processes of the unfolding of the universe. In other words, we do magic.

The Magical Pact, then, consists of Illuminates of this 'Thanateros', with our intentional, willed participation in this densely woven drama of arising and passing away, this Inward-Outward Theatre, this IOT.

What of 'Illuminate'? Pete Carroll himself long ago eschewed any ideas of spiritual illumination, seeing in them the sort of disempowering fantasies that provoked the arising of chaos magic in the first place. And more than one of my colleagues seem quite happy getting rich and laid with no interest in the initiatory tradition that began with our shamanic forebears who, in their view, were chosen by the spirits to deal with them on behalf of the tribe.

At one level, then, 'Illuminate' refers simply to one who apprehends and takes willing, intentional part in this Thanateros of which I've spoken. And indeed, exploring Thanateros as a magician proves a massive adventure which lights up and transforms my entire life. However, there can come a point where I, the magician, increasingly recognise myself(s) as a cluster of interwoven processes of Thanateros and perhaps nothing more.

At this point I'm going to get a little controversial. Not everyone likes the scent of this particular part of my garden. As far as I can tell, by researching my experience, once bitten by the serpent, chosen by the spirits, hit by the initial realization—however you describe it—I find myself on a one-way trip leading to what some call 'enlightenment', which means the same thing as 'illumination' but has extra connotations that have given it an unnecessary aura of specialness and conventional morality. Pursuing this trip takes one through stages of a process known to many traditions worldwide and described by them in eerily similar terms throughout history. In the West we know it as 'The Great Work of Magic'.

In my view, when we do more than dabble in magic, we sign ourselves up for the Great Work, which then takes over more and more if we let it. The Great Work, not our puny selves, runs the show, just as the spirits choose the shaman. But to fail to carry it through leads to disaster. Better not begun; once begun, better to finish. In the Pact we call our taking part in this process by the Ouranian Barbaric expression CHOYOFAQUE, which means 'doing the Great Work of Magic.' We use this expression with each other often, which indicates its importance to us, at whatever level we understand it.

Therefore at this stage let's pause again, this time to bring to mind 'Doing the Great Work of Magic.' Breathe in deeply, and say deliberately: 'CHOYOFAQUE.' Aah, that's better.

And we have arrived at the centre of my labyrinth. Still got the thread? Let me remind you: The Magical Pact of the Illuminates of Thanateros. Now we unravel it back up to emerge from the labyrinth and into the ordinary world. We bring our insights and our illumination to the surface and contribute, as our shamanic forebears did, to our supportive subculture and to the wider world. This contribution, this sharing of the gifts from Otherworld, we sometimes describe as 'immanentizing the Eschaton'. It's a long story. Suffice to say we have an Ouranian Barbaric expression for that too, which we may use as a war cry to drive us on our way. It is: AEPALIZAGE! You know what to do, yes? So, for the last time:

Take a deep breath as you bring to mind the nature of the Pact, and say deliberately: 'GOBCHURINOR FOUIJA.'

Pause and let yourself feel the difference.

Take a deep breath as you bring to mind 'Doing the Great Work of Magic,' and say deliberately: 'CHOYOFAQUE.'

Pause and let yourself feel the difference.

Now take a deep breath as you think of bringing your magic into the world, and exclaim loudly: 'AEPALIZAGE!'

And so it is done.

Enhancing Your Portfolio: Facts and Fictions

Frater Tarod

A magician shares this with entrepreneurs: see the world and change the world. And just like an entrepreneur, if your endeavours are not profitable you are in the shit.

Your portfolio of investments, comprised of actions and beliefs, should serve to better you. Profit you. Develop you. Enhance your life. Improve your experience. Allow you to do more. You get the idea. Investments which do not perform should be cut.

Why the business talk? Because the world provides performance feedback: profit, loss, expense; capacity; resistance, and you will gain from using it. If your actions are not delivering desired results, change them. If your beliefs are not delivering desired results, change them. You owe no loyalty to weak investments and weak returns on those investments. Feedback can be grounded in what is true regardless of your opinion of it.

Example: If your eating habit neglects certain key acquisitions required for high level performance, hampering your efforts in other spheres of life, then your eating habit needs to change. Say you eat raw greens exclusively. You're getting vitamins and minerals but no macros. Your body shrivels up. This makes you sad. Literally. And weak. Literally. You change your eating habit. You add in macros. You feel happy. You grow strong. Your portfolio has improved. Your life has improved.

However, a purely factual approach is not enough. We seem to need the addition of personal meaning. This is expressed in the artworks we create, the quests we undertake, the stories we tell with our rituals of symbolic actions, and with the narratives of our lives.

Best practice demands both facts and fictions. Without our fictions we risk living in a meaningless universe. Without facts, we live in fantasy, with no anchor to the real, and suffer the consequences for it.

Reality does not care about our superstitions. Those that value falsely pay the cost and those that value truthfully reap the reward. It is incumbent then upon the magician to familiarise oneself with and engage with and put into practice both the active acquisition of new facts upon which to base decisions and the active acquisition of new and greater degrees of skill through which to better perform one's will.

A tree speaks...
Sator Syzygy

I recently attended a meeting of the Council of All Beings, a Deep Ecology practice which aims to embody the emotional awareness of our current environmental situation. A dozen of us took part, and spent the afternoon making masks and tuning in to the particular organisms which had chosen to appear through us, before meeting deep in the woods at the twilight hour to talk to some humans:

I am a tree. An Acacia tree, of the African savannah. I speak for all my kind, and for trees in general.

I stand and life comes to me. Big cats rest in my branches, birds perch, dropping nutrients for other plants and creatures who nestle beneath and around me. Giraffes eat leaves from between my long thorns, with tongues specially long and twisty to reach between them. Fierce ants help protect me; they live in specially adapted thorns, which swell to accommodate them, making their houses in my defences.

Sun falls, so hot. Some of my family are chopped up to make fires, by humans; why the need to create more heat when all is so hot already? I do not understand this.

Some acacias provide food for humans. Our seeds in particular are highly nutritious. Our bodies give medicines, perfumes, gums, our bark is rich in tannins; we make timber for furniture, tools, musical instruments. So much matter, so many wondrous ways to transform!

We give so much to human people, as well as to the other peoples of this vast landscape, and they bring so much to us.

This relationship, this interweaving, is the heart of our existence. We make a flat plain extend into another dimension, give height and shade. I love to grow into shapes which flow around the broken parts of me, when an animal knocks or claws a small part away. This is my art. To grow in response to my history, my life story. This twist in my branch, is a lion jumping after a leopard's catch 23 years ago. The asymmetric shape of my crown is an elephant visit, six years past. The circular bulge in my trunk is from a snapped branch in my youth, when weaver bird nests were so heavy it broke. These shapes are my memories. My joy is to adapt, to grow strong around these times. My memories only exist as these physical remains. I have no other way of recalling past events. I have no imagined future. Only Now, an eternal moment, sensing shifting light and shade, of wind moving me, of water filling me, of roots pulling in minerals. Carbon enters through my leaves, and I make wood from thin air.

So many of my ideas I cannot put into words. You must remember, words are not present for any other creatures. Yet, we think and reason with chemicals just like you, who are our relations; our sense of total presence in the here & now can be shared by you if used wisely.

I never move from this spot I took root in. I touch the trees near me, through under the ground networks, and by catching airborne messages.

Our way of living has worked since before the continents separated. Acacia trees have co-evolved with many other organisms, each shaping the other, flowing behaviours, functionality, and materials between us. Some say we may have shaped your people, giving you words and ideas with our medicines; I do not know. I am just a tree, growing.

My gift to you, humans, is an example of how to flourish in a potentially harsh world.

The above text was written after I went to a weekend moot of chaos magicians, where amongst other things a Council of All Beings was held. Thanks to all those present, especially the facilitators of this powerful ritual.

Invisibilism
Frater Sigurd

I've sometimes been asked how I got into magic, and I've given various answers, but the most honest of them is that magic got into me. I remember telling a friend when I was about seven years old that he should be careful around me because, you know, I have magic powers. When he asked me what they were I told him I was still working that out, but that I was totally sure I had them. I spent hours staring at small objects trying to move them with my mind, but never managed to acquire an infallible technique. I had a eureka moment when I worked out that people had got it wrong when they tried to fly by flapping their arms—the secret must be to flap your legs! When I played hide and seek I'd 'hide' in the middle of the room with my eyes tightly closed trying to think nothing at all. To be unseen, I believed, I simply had to do my best to not be there. The seeker would pretend they hadn't seen me, probably because they didn't want to hurt my feelings. No doubt they thought I was an idiot. No doubt I was. But it's also true that making it clear to people that you don't want to be found, persuading them to behave as though you are unfindable, could be a way of achieving something like real invisibility…

Many years later I got into the occult—first the runes, then Peter Carroll, then everything else—and I've loved every minute of it. But recently I've begun to wonder what a magical practice based on my childhood intuitions about magic might look like—a practice structured around the shameless acquisition and development of magic powers. What might it mean to take magic powers powers seriously? If we can't fly by flapping our legs then what's the next best thing? We might not be able to stop time, but might we be able to do something like it...? Below are some incomplete thoughts relating to the power of invisibility, but my ultimate aim is to create a grimoire that includes fleshed-out programmes for obtaining and refining the fundamental magical powers: invisibility, superhuman strength, flight, seduction and psychokinesis. The study of these powers is not affiliated to any mytho-magickal paradigm. The process will assist any serious magickian in doing their will, whether they're into Chaos Magick, Thelema, the Northern Tradition or Gnostic Voudon.

OSTLING IN BOHEMIA

The first thing to ask yourself when thinking about becoming invisible is: whom do I want to be unable to see me? Is it enough for them not to be able to see *me*, or do I need to be completely invisible? Blagging your way into some aristo's party in order to recover a magical talisman stolen by one of his ancestors requires quite a different set of skills to breaking into a battery chicken farm to destroy their machinery. If it's only important that whomever you're trying to fool doesn't see *you*, then all you have to do is be someone else. You need to become a master of disguise. This is not a matter simply of dressing up in someone else's clothes.

In stories such as 'A Scandal in Bohemia', Sherlock Holmes demonstrates the versatility required to be a true master of disguise. Early in the story Holmes disguises himself as a stable groom: he wears 'disreputable clothes' and 'ill-kempt side whiskers', the uniform of the stereotype he's out to imitate, but he also alters his voice and the way he moves. His aim is to get information out of a bunch of ostlers, confident in the knowledge that they'll give it to him because 'there is a wonderful sympathy and freemasonry between horsey men'. But in order to convince them that he is indeed a horsey man he needs to act like them, and to know what they know. He approaches them with an offer to help rub down their horses; in order to do that he had to know how to rub down a horse. Later in the same story, Holmes disguises himself as a clergyman. This demands not only another change of costume, but another set of behaviours, a different accent, a different way of moving through space.

The art of disguising yourself as someone else has much in common with the arts of invocation and evocation. Here is Jan Fries on his first attempt at communicating with Anubis, the Egyptian jackal god:

"First I painted a stele, showing Anpu in the traditional Egyptian style, seated, and in profile. Then followed a time of invocation and ceremony, to charge the painting with a lot of passion and power, the energy to get the magick going. Work with the imagination followed. Whenever I had a spare moment I would recall the picture on the stele and imagine it as clear and as vivid as I could." (*Visual Magick*, 1992)

This is exactly the kind of thing you need to do to get good at disguise, but instead of doing it with a god you must do it with an ostler, or a duke, or a footballer, or a nurse. Think about the person you want to 'become' in detail, and for as long as you can before that person is due to go out into the world. Think about their daily routine, their family life, their likes and dislikes, their sexual proclivities. The more you know about your character the better able you'll be to pass yourself off as them. A good way of building up a character (this works with invocation and evocation too) is by working with a partner and asking each other questions. What is your favourite colour? Why did your second wife divorce you? And so on. When starting out with this kind of invisibility it's best to choose a character who is like you in many respects; it's easier to change a few things than many. As you get better at it, you can begin working with more exotic personalities.

Here's an exercise. Begin by picking a football team. (I can't work out whether this works better if you actually like football and pick a team you despise, or if, like me, you're not into football at all.) Learn everything you can about the team: the names of the players, the position they're in in the league, who they've played, the history of the club. Pick a name for your character and work out where they're from, then work out some of your character's family history, especially his/her reasons for supporting the team you've chosen. Was it the local team? Did your dad support them? Then pick a sports pub in the vicinity of the football club you're going to be pretending to support. Go there on match day dressed in the appropriate football strip. Make friends . . .

ELEMENTAL MANOEUVRES IN THE DARK

Breaking into a chicken farm is different. You don't want to be seen at all. Magickians who are interested in this kind of working might want to consider learning some ninjutsu, the art of stealth developed by Japanese warriors in the 7th century. Ninjutsu enables its practitioners to spy on their enemies, and to penetrate enemy strongholds, without being seen. Fundamental to ninjutsu is inpo, the art of hiding. Again, there are strong correlations between inpo and classic Western occult practices, particularly the invocation of elements. In inpo there are five different styles of hiding, and each of them (bar one) is inspired by one of the elements. Before practising any of these styles you may find it useful to perform a simple elemental invocation. (If you're practising on real enemies in the field, do it in your head—being inaudible is the second rule of ninjutsu after being invisible.)

The Earth method of hiding is based on the principle that if you completely fill the space between two objects then the eyes of anyone looking for you will pass over you, because you are embedded so harmoniously into the landscape. Think of using holes, or the gaps between rocks, or the spaces below bushes and shrubs. The space should be big enough for you to fit into it, but no bigger: you become invisible by melding with the earth itself. This technique can of course be improved with a disguise. We often think of ninjas romping around in all-black costumes, but they more often dressed in grey, or brown, or red. Before practising the Earth method think about what kind of terrain you're going to be working with, and, especially, what kind of light there will be. If you're working in daylight, in a forest, a brown costume may be more appropriate. If it's nighttime I recommend grey. The most important thing about disguise in inpo is to wear clothes that are soft, and that fit well. Starchy clothing makes too much noise, and baggy clothing can easily get caught on branches and thorns. It is a terrible thing to have your clothes unravel on a mission, and to be caught butt-naked in the floodlamps of the enemy!

The Water style of inpo involves concealing yourself in water so as to erase your trail. A word of warning: use it in the dark only; water is transparent and therefore not well-suited to hiding. If you absolutely have to practise the water technique in daylight then combine it with the Earth technique and obscure your body with mud, boulders or bullrushes. The Water method is often used to set a trap. Immerse yourself in river, marsh, lake or pond. As soon as the enemy charges into the water to look for you they become vulnerable: they lose sight of your tracks and their footing is suddenly precarious. Let them take a few steps before dragging them down into the water and drowning them. (Only kill enemies in a life-or-death situation; it's usually enough merely to render them unconscious.)

The Fire method comprises mastery of light and shade. The most obvious principle here is to make sure you are always behind a light source, so that you don't cast a shadow. It is not advisable to use a torch when you are some distance away from the enemy as the movement of light can give away your location. But at close range a powerful light can be a useful weapon, and, indeed, a good way of preserving your invisibility. In a woodland confrontation, suddenly illuminating a large lamp will dazzle your foe giving you time to escape, or to dodge past them. Use smoke, too, if you want: it freaks people out and disappearing in a puff of smoke feels very wizardly. You can buy a decent smoke grenade these days online for about a tenner. Fire style is also concerned with ways of moving, but I'll talk a bit more about that after treating the remaining elements.

The so-called Air method involves hiding higher than the foe's line of sight—up a tree for example. People look down and straight ahead more often than they look up. If you're in a tree, hug it tightly so that if your enemy does look up he or she is less likely to see you. Silent gliding—accessing a hill fort by parachuting into it from above, say—also belongs to the air method. On landing, however, you will often need to flow immediately into what is known as the 'Wood' method (the one method without an elemental basis, though I've also seen it referred to as the 'void' method, which I suppose correlates loosely with 'spirit'). This is the trickiest as it involves hiding without cover, distorting your silhouette so that you no longer look human. It's most effective by night. One classic pose is the boulder: you curl yourself up into a ball, as tightly as you can, and hope the foe mistakes you for a large stone. It's a pretty desperate manoeuvre. Bizarrely, one of the most effective postures associated with the Wood method is a yogic headstand. The enemy will be looking for a human shape: head on top, then torso, then legs. The headstand is the best way of very quickly altering your shape into something very different. In the dark the enemy will see two fronds—your legs—gently wavering in the breeze. He or she may mistake them for a pair of ostriches, or birch saplings, but will be unlikely to see them as human: for one thing it simply won't have occurred to them that you would do something as ridiculous as pulling a headstand while they're looking for you, so they'll see your headstand as anything but that. You will have been protected by your own preposterousness, which is always satisfying.

Inpo is combined with the art of stealthy movement known as Kuji Ashi, the Nine Steps. These are the classic set of movements that the ninja uses in order to move without giving him or herself away. There are nine of these, obviously, and each step has its rules. It's worth looking them up. There are steps that are incredibly slow and silent—so slow that you're supposed not to be able to tell that the ninja is moving at all. There are steps that are intended for movement at speed, and ones that minimise the silhouette. There are crawling steps and variations on the classic tip-toe. But it's pointless getting bogged down in form unless you want to become a ninjutsu master. Chaos Magick is all about results, and what you really want to do is develop a movement, or set of movements, in collaboration with your coven, by thinking about the kinds of terrain you're going to be tackling. Practise together, and your coven mates will be able to tell you whether or not they can see you, or whether you're making a sound or not. Ninjas carry around a sash belt, or obi, that they can put on the floor when they need to cross gravel silently— something like that could be useful. Here are a few other pointers: when walking upstairs keep close to the wall to minimise creaking; never pass a mirror openly; always be aware of your own shadow; carry wire cutters for barbed wire.

TALES FROM THE ENCRYPT

I'm going to flout compositional logic now by ending on the least exciting kind of invisibility— invisibility on the internet. I won't go into too much detail, because there's a lot of it online and it can be found with ease—but I will say that evading internet surveillance is an absolutely crucial skill for the serious modern magickian. The internet, especially the Dark Web, has much to offer, including obscure sacraments, potion ingredients and magical weapons. It also provides an effective means of attacking your magical enemies. You can probably do more damage to a banking corporation these days by hacking into its servers and stealing or erasing data than you can by breaking into their offices ninja-style. Hacking also doesn't involve immersing yourself in cold pond water, or snagging your onesie on barbed wire. If you're going to use the internet for magical purposes, however, you absolutely must become unseeable. As we all know now, thanks largely to Edward Snowden, our governments can and do monitor our online activity constantly. Just because you can't see them, that doesn't mean they're not there.

Here, then, is a brief list of the absolute basics of online invisibility. Put these imperatives into practise immediately. It's easy to do so and you won't regret it.

Don't use Windows. Don't use Google.

Use Tor (and the Tor browser), a free piece of software that protects you from traffic analysis by disguising your IP address.

Use a VPN (Virtual Private Network). Most VPNs do not keep records of your online activity, so aren't susceptible to government requests. They also disguise your location.

When using Tor online for magical purposes do not download browser plugins (such as Flash) or open downloaded documents with the browser still open. Doing either of these things can give away your IP address.

Use Bitcoin to make your transactions untraceable.

Encrypt your computer (using, for example, TrueCrypt) to prevent hackers from accessing it, and encrypt your keystrokes (using Keyscrambler) to stop them from reading what you type.

There's much more to online invisibility—and if you're going to take down a banking corp I hope you do your research—but those points should be enough to secure you a dead man's toe, or a Glock, or a kilo of rare hashish, without getting busted. Remember, nothing is real and everything is permitted—but you'll still have to deal with the consequences of your actions. Not all cops wear blue.

Get Laid, Get Rich, Get Even

Frater Modus

Morals and ethics are not topics usually covered when talking about Chaos Magic. Emphasis generally is on results, from where comes one of the usual critiques to this system I like the most.

More than once I have heard that Chaos Magicians are only interested in three things: to get laid, to get rich, and to get even. With this it is said that we are a bunch of egotistical self-centred people with no interest on what is known as Illumination or, at a more ground level, even the consequences of our actions.

I agree completely with morals and ethics not being usually discussed in the system, because this lack serves, in my view, an important function.

From the very beginnings of this metaparadigm or metamodel known as Chaos Magic the objective has been to analyse the old illumination and magical systems from a non-sectarian perspective, attempting to separate the wheat from the chaff.

A moral system is a frame for action inside of which we move, and as such a tool to lean on and decide the best way to carry on our actions Moral systems used to be inherited, and they depend in great measure on culture and education.

When they are not backed by experience, these moral systems have a tendency to become chains rather than frames, generating all kinds of prejudices. If the hows or whys of a moral system are not put into question, a moral system is just a brainwash we are subject to because we have been told is the right thing to do, because this is what the people who know do. This is why it is better to know by oneself, so that our personal moral code is wheat, and not chaff.

Examining the previously cited cliché:

TO GET LAID

If we think this literally, sex is a natural impulse, and very pleasurable, so why not exploring it according to our tastes?

If we look at this from a wider perspective we can understand it as getting what we want. If we spend a little time analysing our motivations and the result of our actions we are going to get to a better knowledge of said motivations, of ourselves, and of our relation with others. When you manage to manifest a wish, it usually manifests what Buddhists call The First Noble Truth, being, more or less, that to crave is to suffer. Do I mean with this that life is shit and there is no satisfaction but to suppress our wishes so we get free of the moral and emotional tensions they subject us to? No, what I mean is that when an objective is reached we immediately find objections, or it manifests in a way we didn't want, or that consequences go beyond our predictions. Every time we make something happen it is inevitable to gather data about ourselves, how we see reality, what we want, what we think we want, how we relate and connect with people... which invites us to put in question our own moral code and view.

Using the word from an Occidental perspective, it illuminates us, sheds light over the matter.

TO GET RICH

Having developed the previous point it not very necessary to go into much detail with this one, because here too getting what you want takes you to newer perspectives on what that means exactly, or even what does wanting something mean. It makes us think too on our relation with material stuff and what do riches mean for us; if it means money, pleasure, a quiet life, adventure...

TO GET EVEN

The celebrated destruction of our enemies. "What is best in life?" Conan style (presumably paraphrased from Genghis Khan):

Khitan General: My fear is that my sons will never understand me... Hao! Dai ye! We won again! This is good. But what is best in life?

Khitan Warrior: The open steppe, a fleet horse, falcons at your wrist, and the wind in your hair.

Khitan General: Wrong! Conan, what is best in life?

Conan: To crush your enemies, see them driven before you, and to hear the lamentations of their women!

Khitan General: ...That is good.

We can go to the literal again, to the "I'm going to step over your dead body", or the "I am going to destroy you because it is your fault I failed the Maths exam", or we can dig a bit more. This third point holds how we manage with concepts like justice, guilt, or empathy. They are very profound ideas with great implications in our daily lives, so having a look at them from time to time can be beneficial.

When I say to question or to put something to the test I am not talking about throwing our ethics and morals to the bin to be replaced by a shiny nothing.

That is only one of the paradigms you can visit.

Each paradigm has its own moral system or systems, each with its own forms of understanding the world and our interactions with it. Explore different ethical codes. That's what the tools of paradigm shifting are for.

Now, if during that exploration you are considering doing something that can bring you nefarious consequences, or that you will most likely regret soon, then think twice. It is better to study the objective in advance. That's what your logic, common sense, and the tools of divination are for.

As a general rule do not act in the heat of the moment. That's when we often make the worst decisions. To use the great power of emotions is what the tools of trance are for.

Summing up, the construction of our own ethical code is, from my perspective, one of the fundamental pieces in the consecution of The Great Work. To assimilate other's code without question is to become its slave, and to question your own helps get you free from your own chains, or at least to be more free to choose the chains that you like more, or are more interesting to you.

Remembering the Elephant

Sator Syzysy

When I was a young magician, in my twenties, I was curious about lived religious experience. In the culture I inhabited, religion—by which I mean engagement with the eternal/non-rational ways of thinking about the world—was limited to Christian church approved systems. Spending Sunday morning standing in a draughty old building weighed down by centuries of state oppression did not appeal to me (a mother of two young children, whose hobby was playing bass guitar for an all-female punk band). As a Classical scholar I was well aware of the Olympian mythology, and as a fan of storytelling I knew something about the Norse epic poems, tales and characters. However, these were from societies which are no longer extant, and offered little in regard to experiencing what I sought, a religion of the Now.

As a chaos magician I decided to look to a culture with a still living tradition which I felt I could contact the vibrant spirit of. I chose Hindu deities; as a virtual subject of the British Empire (I grew up with a pre-war copy of the *Encyclopedia Brittanica* as my source of world history; no Wikipedia in those days!) I felt a familiarity with the Indian subcontinent.

Nowadays I would have concerns about cultural appropriation, but in the 1990s this phrase was unheard of. So I merrily embarked upon my quest, to make contact with a pantheon of non-extinct gods and goddesses.

The process of making acquaintance with these new figures took me many years. I started with Ganesh, of course (he is always called upon at the start of any enterprise, as a propitious act), and after a full length puja (for which I memorised a third of the titles, so I could recite them by heart) I did a daily small puja to an icon I got. The icon is a painting from India, small and perfectly formed, with the stars in the sky picked out in gold. I lit incense, greeted the icon, and bowed before it at the start of every day for a couple of years. When not at home I used a photograph of the icon on my mobile phone.

This coincided with a period of regular yoga practice, and further investigations into Hinduism. To cut a long story short, twenty years later I have icons of Durga, Lakshmi and Sarasvati, of Shiva and Vinayaki (an elephant headed goddess), and a statue of Ganesh. I learned several mantras, and gained insights into Kali in particular, as well as other cultural learnings; mudras, offerings, memory techniques, the history of India, the caste structure, modern day aspects (e.g. digital images are considered valid as icons); I visited the temple in Wimbledon for a major puja to Ganesh, dressed appropriately, and took offerings of milk and sweets. We were made very welcome by the people there. I was pleased to find a statue of Hanuman, the monkey god, lurking in the corridor at the back of the main Ganesh shrine. The sounds of chanting, smells of incense and foods, the swirling colourful mass of beautiful clothes, flowers, gold jewellery and garlands, was deeply overwhelming to the senses and the mind was filled with the ceremony, pushing out any other concerns.

This practice formed a periodic strand to my magical workings. It is only one of the areas I have encountered, but I wanted to share the way that choosing to engage in one paradigm, for specific reasons, has resulted in a lot of outcomes.

On one level I have learnt a little about the Indian subcontinent. I feel closer to this part of the world for doing this, despite never having visited it. I feel I did contact the living reality of these gods, some of them appeared in various visions, and my prayers to them are to real entities, whom I feel real emotions for. By sharing religious ceremony, even remotely, we enjoy a kindred bond that provides an emotional strength to any ongoing relationship.

So now, I am contacting the spirits of the land I move upon. All the planet is connected, but it would be ridiculous to ignore the fact that parts of it are identifiable. So here I am, with the sky above me, the earth beneath me, the waters embracing this island, and a fire within my heart. I have clues and whispered echoes of the names of the gods and goddesses, the spirits of this place; yet these are delicate words, faint traces at best. How can I possibly truly connect with that which we have had ripped away from us?

The answer is, I cannot. All I can do is to build up from the remains; clearing away the dust of ages to reveal what I can find as elemental foundations. The earth, water, air and fire, wood and flesh. Animals and plants of specific natures. Weather conditions. By poetic metaphor, out of relational structures, as I walk across landscapes and learn of how human animals lived here in ages past, from the patterns of life we can still find if we know how and where to look. By combining this material of the past with an appreciation of the present, flavoured by historical systems along the way, perhaps I can be a part of a religious (again, in the sense of engagement with the eternal/non-rational ways of thinking about the world) movement. We need to feel emotional connection with the immediate, with those who lived before, and, with those who will live afterwards. This for me is the Great Work of my life. By this connecting, we can motivate ourselves and our groups to take a kindlier view towards all things, which seems to me to lie at the root of a successful way of existing which does not simply exploit.

Chaos Magick has a reputation for being a dangerous activity. My own tiny story above, reflecting only one part of my magical journey, might demonstrate just how powerful this choosing of beliefs can become. It motivated me to do a degree in ecology, to start a career in publishing, and to volunteer as helper with several projects I felt moved to. My path is only beginning; each day brings fresh adventures to this foundational project of mine. I meet others whose own quests relate to it, and we hug and smile as we recognise that in each other; sometimes we talk overtly about it, often we get to actual business matters.

There are many ways in which people choose to engage with the spiritual, the magical, the eternal, the numinous. Some can appear, at first glance, as straightforward, or downright peculiar. The glamours we dress in as magicians take all sorts of forms. Whether a person works with crystals or whips, they have a deeper passion and that is what is worth exploring. Chaos Magic allows those of all kinds of paradigms and metaparadigms to talk as equals, to demonstrate techniques as they mutually decide to. It has enormous power to spread ways of being in the world far and wide, and to inspire new ways.

My magical journeys of exploration have taken me to historical Nordic and Mediterranean Europe, ancient Middle Eastern kingdoms; contemporary North American ceremonies, African possession states (via Haiti) and South American group vigils. With brief excursions to the Far East, to the islands of the Pacific, frozen Finnish huts and desert gatherings of nomads, forest dwellers and seashore settlements. Visiting these placetimes in a virtual sense, rather than physical, nevertheless evokes a far greater awareness and appreciation of them than any amount of book reading; by meeting those people who have been there, who share the ways these groups celebrate and engage with their communities, provides a tangible awareness of them as real, living, breathing men and women.

Meeting those who practise versions of witchcraft and pagan, druidic, or other Western styles of magic, helps to understand what kind of things have appealed to those who live near me (in time and place). However 'true' these belief systems may be, they do show what many thousands of people currently feel drawn to. These ideas of how we might recognise the turning of the wheel of the year by celebrating in locally particular ways provide an architecture of potential future traditions. Each year, newspapers include ever more of this kind of festival, often based upon a seed of historical evidence, but nevertheless flowering into a living manifestation of connection with a past and therefore a future, helping us stand outside our individual span and to understand how our acts impact on far more than we will ever perceive.

I weep for my own ancestors, whose religions were deleted by, well, I don't even know what to blame. I wept a few nights ago, for the keepers of wisdom through the ages, passing on what they could by means overt and covert. Scraps and rags of the clothing that once adorned my many times great grandparents. Today, I am one member of a huge search party looking for ways of creating ceremony, creating ritual, for reasons of healing, creativity, bonding, enjoyment, learning, opening up our tiny selves to the bigger picture. By doing ceremony from other places, I can see examples of superstructures from elsewhere which can help guide the forms I construct to guide the flows of attention, of intention, of results. The Pact of the IOT as a group of people provides a microcosm for trying out ways to do this, a capable group not shy with feedback and criticism, a tribe of friends and acquaintances, all of whom have a high level of self-control, self-expression, and passion.

I count my lucky stars that I became part of them so early in my life; I would not be half the person I am without them.

I look at people and I see a consciousness I share looking back at me from all eyes. I see it in the feathered dinosaurs in the hedgerows, the amphibians and reptiles, the fishes of clear streams. I stand before a tree, and the muscles of my feet and legs adjust to mirror its stance. By recognising myself in all around me, I begin to act as a conduit for Life, saying the words and doing the things which my environment moves me to.

But, that piece of philosophy is a whole other story.

To be continued...

I close my essay as any good magician does, with a banishing. May the ground rise up to meet your feet, may you never thirst, may the wind blow at your back, may the sun shine upon your deeds and fire brighten your hearth. May your gods go with you.

Jai Ganesh!

Nothing is True, Everything is Permitted

www.iotbritishisles.org

www.thanateros.org

Printed in Great Britain
by Amazon